KU-108-204

RSA LIBRARY

WITHDRAWN

07252

EDUCATION AND WARFARE IN EUROPE

Education and Warfare in Europe

DAVID COULBY
Bath Spa University College

CRISPIN JONES
University of London Institute of Education

Ashgate

Aldershot • Burlington USA • Singapore • Sydney

© David Coulby and Crispin Jones 2001

All rights reserved. No part of this publication may be reproduced, stored in a retrieval system or transmitted in any form or by any means, electronic, mechanical, photocopying, recording or otherwise without the prior permission of the publisher.

Published by
Ashgate Publishing Limited
Gower House
Croft Road
Aldershot
Hampshire GU11 3HR
England

Ashgate Publishing Company
131 Main Street
Burlington, VT 05401-5600 USA

Ashgate website: http://www.ashgate.com

British Library Cataloguing in Publication Data
Coulby, David
    Education and warfare in Europe
    1.War and education - Europe 2.War and society - Europe
    3.Children and war - Europe 4.Education and state - Europe
    I.Title II.Jones, Crispin
    303.6'6

Library of Congress Control Number: 2001088801

ISBN 0 7546 1204 X

Printed and bound by Athenaeum Press, Ltd.,
Gateshead, Tyne & Wear.

[15440]

Contents

Acknowledgements

Both authors have been lucky enough to have worked with teachers and others across Europe dealing with many of the issues raised in this book. Every encounter has made us challenge our assumptions and ideas about the relationship between education and warfare (and much more besides). We are also grateful for the helpful comments that have been given us by our colleagues, particularly those in the Urban Education Research Group.

The book is dedicated to those who have to make educational decisions about issues concerning knowledge and warfare in educational climates less benign than those in which the two of us work.

> *Peace hath her victories*
> *No less renowned than war*
>   Milton

1 Europe, Education and Warfare

Sarajevo is in many aspects, a typical southern European city. In the evenings, its famous 'walking street' is full of young people and families strolling along, greeting friends, enjoying the feeling of being with other people. Celebrating the very act of being free to walk their streets in safety, an aspect of life most of us in Europe take for granted. Sarajevo is also, in a sense, at the core of this book. Events in the city helped frame the century that has just finished, events that had a decisive impact on European history. In 1914, the spark that ignited the First World War, the assassination of Archduke Franz Ferdinand and his wife, took place in an unremarkable Sarajevo street. No plaque marks the spot. The revenge that the Austro-Hungarian empire took on Serbia at that time was horrendous, 15% of its population dying in the subsequent war, a fact often forgotten amid the more general carnage. The inadequate peace led to the Second World War, which further devastated Europe. And in the 1990s, Sarajevo was back, this time the victim of an horrendous siege by Serbian forces, from which the city is only now, in the next century, recovering.

All over former Yugoslavia, schools were destroyed, teachers and pupils killed, while the rest of Europe looked on, trying to reason away irrationality. The fighting has been stopped, international aid has rebuilt many of the schools and new teachers are being trained. The international community is endeavouring to support new countries like Bosnia-Herzegovina to build up an education system that is both efficient and modern but one that also will play a leading role in the attempt to curb old enmities and build a new generation that will not so readily be the victims and agents of war.

In that ending of violence, as so often in the past, searching questions have been asked of education. What contribution did it make to both starting and stopping the violence? And as so often after wars, the education system is reformed, to rebuild not just the economy but also to try and build the state ('nation') anew.

If major education changes and reforms occur after wars, partly to avoid their re-occurrence, it is important to examine why, in Europe as elsewhere, there has been only partial success in that aim. This is the primary purpose of this book. The book does not assert that education causes wars. Teachers across Europe would, in the main, assert that they

1

endeavour to teach tolerance and respect to their children in their care. It is probable, but improvable, that they have been successful more often than not. Europe has been relatively at peace for the last fifty or so years compared with much of the rest of the world and education has likely played a part in that. However, events in the 1990s have punctured some of that optimism. Can those working in European education systems do more, perhaps by re-examining their policy and practices, to re-build that confidence? This book attempts that process. It tries to tease out why and in what ways, European schools and universities maintain and sustain antipathies, nationalisms and xenophobic attitudes which in turn, have the potential for the initiation of violence and ultimately, war.

The ending of the Cold War was said at the time to be both the 'end of history' (Fukuyama, 1992) and the beginning of the 'peace dividend' as the run down of armed forces around the world meant increased revenues being spent on more socially useful activities like poverty amelioration. The widespread perception that warfare was at an end was based on a view of war as the clash between the armed forces of states along the lines of the First and Second World Wars. Yet warfare has continued after 1991, in Europe as elsewhere. Much of it is classified as either civil wars, 'low intensity warfare' or 'sub-conventional warfare', where state armed forces fight guerrilla or other non-state armed forces. In Europe, such sub-conventional wars are being fought or have been recently fought in, amongst other places, Albania, France, Georgia, Russia (Chechnya), former Yugoslavia and the United Kingdom. Some have been relatively minor for the states involved, Northern Ireland and Corsica for example, although clearly not for the people caught up in the violence. Others, like the conflicts in Georgia and former Yugoslavia, have devastated whole populations.

Europe has been formed by war, as indeed, has much of the world. As Freedman notes:

> Wars have taken place from the beginning of recorded time in all parts of the world. They are prominent, and sometimes dominant, both in history books and today's headlines. They have shaped the international system and prompted social change. They have inspired literature, art and music (Freedman, 1994, p. 3).

Nowhere is this more true than in Europe. The break up of the Roman and Byzantine empires and the slow division of Europe into competing 'nation states' is a process not yet at its end. Meanwhile new supranational organisations like the European Union and, to a lesser extent, the United Nations and the Council of Europe are emerging. Even NATO is falteringly attempting to find itself a more peaceful and less partisan role in maintaining European stability.

However, the last 200 years have seen Europe dominated and sometimes decimated by war. The French and American revolutions introduced the idea of citizen armies and the obligation for males to fight for their country as opposed to being forced to fight for their rulers. The new citizen armies were defending their own rights, not just those of their princes. Lloyd George, the British Prime Minister put it succinctly in 1918, '...the story of democracy is this: no democracy has ever long survived the failure of its adherents to be ready to die for it' (Quoted in Terraine, 2000, p. 45). And die they did. Shortly after this speech, in the fighting on the Western Front, some 700,000 Europeans became battle casualties in just forty days, - 17,500 per day (p. 67), a far higher rate of loss than even the battles of the Somme and Passchendaele.

During the Revolutionary and Napoleonic wars the nature of warfare changed. Wars were no longer fought between armies or princes or even governments but between peoples. There were two further concomitants of this. Firstly, whole economies could be devoted to war in peacetime as well as during conflict. Economy became a means of warfare either in Napoleon's Continental System aiming to cut off supplies to the maritime UK or in Churchill's gearing of the entire UK economy to the production of war materials after 1939. Secondly, since whole economies were at war, whole populations came to be seen to be at war. Civilians became increasingly the targets and casualties of war. The Great War resulted largely in military casualties. On the eastern front of the Great Patriotic War there were far more civilian casualties than military. A trend which increased in Korea and Vietnam.

The growth of the citizen army in the 19th and 20th centuries was an integral part of the industrialising, colonising and competing world of European states. European armies became larger and better armed, fuelled and financed by the industrial growth experienced by Europe during the 19th and 20th centuries. Towards the end of the 19th century, conscription ensured that most young European males went on from school to do military service. Indeed, mass education and conscription developed alongside one another. The new industrial states needed more efficient and educated workers and citizens. And a key part of that duty of citizenship was the obligation of males to be prepared to fight for their country and for women to sustain them in that task. In this process, education played a leading role.

Throughout this book the case is being put forward that education systems, in particular but not exclusively those of Europe, far from being oppositional to violence and the horrors of war, are in practice more ambiguous in their stance towards what most people would see as evils. The focus is not on education systems that explicitly glorify war, such as that of Nazi Germany (Pine, 1997a and b) but more on those whose organisers think that they oppose and discourage all aspects of violence (though see the discussion of knowledge and prejudice in Chapter Five). This would describe that of England and indeed, those of most of the other systems in Europe.

Further, the majority of teachers in Europe would claim to be oppositional to warfare and insist that their teaching reflects this. The actuality is more complex (and involves also the role of youth movements, the theme of Chapter Seven). At best, educational systems can attempt to limit the potential for conflict but can seldom prevent it. Indeed, the expansion and increasing sophistication of education systems can unwittingly increase the potential for warfare rather than the reverse. The increasing domination of the free market, coupled with globalisation, has led to increasing competition between states and within states for the distribution of resources, including education. This competition is between rich and poor, between ethnic, religious and linguistic groups and between men and women. A key resource in this trade is in so called 'defence', the sale and distribution of offensive weapons which helps sustain the economies of states like the UK, France, Russia, the USA and even South Africa, while at the same time serving to impoverish and destabilise the states that purchase them. Recent attempts to create an 'ethical foreign policy' by the British Government to change this state of affairs have had limited success, with economic interests taking precedence over the cutting off of armaments to dubious regimes. There is a distortion here of the benefits that science and technology can potentially bring to society. The development of a transmission/suspension system, for instance, that can hold a tank gun steady over rough ground has yet to be applied to ambulances that travel over speed bumps, owing to its cost. Such technological distortion and the trade it engenders throughout Europe and the rest of the world is seldom discussed in the school curriculum, despite its political and economic importance and relevance to the young student. Yet the technology of the warfare industry is itself taught in European schools and universities.

The arms trade is free market competition at perhaps its most unpleasant but it is also symptomatic of the competition that is increasingly seen by most European political parties as the basis for both economic and social development, including educational development. As such, the importance of competition is increasingly being seen as one of the most important factors within an education system. Young people have to be given the skills and tools so that they can compete for the often limited resources found in or provided by the state. Such competition for educational and other resources within states was traditionally seen in class terms and the inequalities caused by this have been investigated in education and other social policy areas for much of the last century. The strengths and weaknesses of such an approach are well exemplified in Karabel and Halsey's anthology (Karabel and Halsey, 1977). Still powerful in much of their explanatory power, such works were increasingly criticised and alternatives offered from the 1970s onwards. Alternative, or more properly, additional explanations were offered, gender and race/ethnicity being two of the more significant, giving rise to a considerable educational literature by the late 1990s (e.g. Sammons, 1994). What the better of these studies showed was the relative permanence of inequalities over time and the modest influence of education on social mobility. One consequence of this is that explanations of inequality, real or imaginary, become part of a group's culture and shared history, with the potential for further reinforcing divisions within a state. These 'hidden' community histories are important, a point taken up later in this book. They are a significant response to the way in which group rights are espoused or denied by education systems and need to be examined for their potential for both violence and, more positively, for conflict resolution.

In a similar way, the conflict resolution potential of education has to be made more explicit and more realistic. Religious or Marxist platitudes about the love between all peoples put forward by education systems are generally treated as they deserve. They characteristically do little to counter xenophobic or other hostilities within the student body. This is not, at this stage, to attack either religion or Marxism or to deny their continuing importance (Gundara, 1997). Religion has sometimes been a powerful progressive force in European education and has espoused the educational rights of oppressed peoples, as Hickman's work on the Roman Catholic church in relation to the Irish in the UK demonstrates (Hickman, 1996). Such belief systems retain their hold over vast numbers of people. The rise of the Communist Party as well as the increase in Orthodox Christian belief in post-USSR Russia and the fact that more adults in the USA trust Genesis rather than Darwin substantiates this (Vallely, 1997). The tension between religious views on violence, perhaps best exemplified by discussions about the nature of the 'just war', is an educational theme running through this book. It is a significant aspect of the tensions between the sometimes conflicting knowledges and values of the school and those of many students that are a feature of much contemporary education in Europe. As such they are a source of a real potential for conflict rather than conflict resolution.

So, what is the education system's role in this continuing propensity to violence? The main point being made in this book is that the curriculum of most European education systems continues to normalise warfare in some form or another. War is seen as barbaric certainly but also as part of the 'natural' order of things. Giddens' view that power is used to conceal sectional interests is helpful here. It means that the dominant discourses, including educational discourse and that about warfare, make common the views of the dominant group, blur contradictions and naturalise the present (Giddens, 1979). Thus, although education systems claim to be against war, at the same time they legitimate it through the use of concepts like the just war.

That there is increasing uneasiness over even this term is revealed by the fact that 'official' wars are now seldom fought. The NATO action against Yugoslavia in relation to atrocities in Kosovo was not officially or legally a war, although the inhabitants of Belgrade may have found such a distinction a little academic. Military violence thus continues, even if is described as 'peacekeeping'.

How schools and other educational institutions respond to the changing pattern of warfare is complex. They have to face a range of complex issues that do not have a simple solution. Amongst the main ones are:

- the idea of a 'just war';
- the teaching of the national literature, a considerable amount of which relates to past wars;
- symbolic remembrance of past wars in such events as Remembrance Day;
- patriotism and love of country;
- the history and demography of the state in which the educational institution is located;
- the geography of the state, especially as it relates to boundaries;
- the language(s) of the state and its/their complex relation to its history and geography.

These issues are discussed in more detail in later chapters. The rest of this chapter looks at them in broad terms, to help shape the arguments and signals the chapters in which they are subsequently developed.

The idea of a 'just war' is a useful place to start this discussion. In schools, simple violence is seen as an activity to be condemned. For example, bullying, an activity endemic in many schools, is seen as a practice that they should combat firmly. Military violence is more difficult. Past wars are taught about in a way which stresses their horror and their wasteful loss of life but at the same time they are frequently presented as 'just wars', for example the struggle against fascism in the Second World War, the Great Patriotic War. In other words, certain military events are seen as justified, especially those in which the individual state was involved. Germany is a clear exception to this general rule in that the Second World War is taught about in a manner that demonstrates the nature of the German regime that participated in it. In most other European states, however, the justness of the military activities seldom explores non-just activities perpetrated by the victorious side, for example the area bombing policy of the Allied air forces (USAF, RAF) in that war, which systematically bombed civilian populations.

The teaching of religion in schools, a commonplace throughout Europe, is pertinent here (It is discussed in detail in Chapter Four). Many established European religions, in particular, have a strong element of support and indeed enthusiasm for just wars. In the Old Testament, the military successes of Israel are seen as being the product of the intimate relationship between Jehovah and the chosen people. Many of the heroes in the Bible are celebrated for their success in battle. The stories of Samson and of David for example are full of detailed accounts of their victories in battle, parallel to other European epics such as *The Iliad* or *Beowulf*. As Samson himself boasted: With the jaw bone of an ass I have heaped them in heaps, with the jaw-bone of an ass I have slain a thousand men (Judges, XV, 16). That relationship between religion and the hero has continued to this day. Although the message of the New Testament is more ambiguous, in that it can be read as being against warfare, considerable effort on the part of theologians to support the idea of a just war has been exerted over the centuries. Moreover, the Islamic concept of the Jihad, a holy or just war, is still invoked. When war occurs, God is always on 'our' side and not on 'theirs', although 'they' may mistakenly believe the opposite.

Yet the dilemma remains about the nature of a just war. In certain circumstances, the recourse to violence is seen not merely as the lesser of two evils but as a positive good, regulated by international law. As Vivienne Jabri notes:

> The doctrine of just war is, however, also constitutive of war. That is, it contains constitutive rules which enable war as a form of conduct and which have, like its regulatory rules, institutionalized war as a social continuity (Jabri, 1996, p. 107).

Thus schools may be left in the complex dilemma of trying to explain when a war is just. In crude terms, it is usually a just war when that state is at war with another or with an element within the state. The sophistication of the debate about the nature of the just war thus quickly descends into another element of support for violence. Further support for such a view is to be found in the teaching of the national literature, a considerable amount of which is concerned with past wars.

The teaching of national literature (discussed in Chapter Four and the theme of Chapter Six) is likely to be more nationalistic, patriotic and xenophobic in wartime. The more interesting issue is its role in peacetime. Certainly, since the ending of the Second World War, the invocation of literature to support struggle has diminished in much of Europe. Newbolt's poetry is thankfully no longer studied save to try and demonstrate how jingoism can get into poetry. The literature of the First World War is studied mainly to demonstrate Wilfred Owen's 'pity of war', rather than its glorification.

How this fits with the majority of the children's view of war, particularly boys, is more problematic in an era of Laura Croft, *Doom*-like 'shoot 'em up' computer games and the never ending stream of new and old war films like *Saving Private Ryan* and *Braveheart*. The overall effect is likely to be to maintain the importance of war in terms of national consciousness and continuity often most powerfully expressed through Symbolic remembrance.

Remembrance Day in Britain, like similar events across Europe, is a classic case of keeping such national continuity alive. Recent moves to drop the event were seen as being completely out of touch with the public mood. Indeed, Remembrance Day is being commemorated more in the last few years, with popular attempts to bring back the minute's silence on November 11th each year. Every year, the famous lines from *For the Fallen* by Lawrence Binyon are solemnly intoned, often in school assemblies:

> They shall not grow old
> As we that are left grow old:
> At the going down of the sun and in the morning
> We will remember them
> (Quoted in Roberts, 1996, p. 56).

The previous verse is less frequently read:

> They went with songs to the battle: they were young,
> Straight of limb, true of eye, steady and aglow.
> They were staunch to the end against odds uncounted:
> They fell with their faces to the foe
> (p. 56).

The interesting question is why such events, which had great poignancy and purpose in post world war periods, maintain their power. The 'never again' argument may have some force but the main purpose still appears to be the privileging of some deaths over others. States and schools do not really commemorate the civilian loss of life in conflict. It is the patriotism of military death which is increasingly the focus of such ceremonies.

Patriotism and love of country is a conundrum. Commemorations of past victories (and sometimes defeats like Kosovo Fields and Dunkirk) have other purposes too and link in with the difficult issue of patriotism, Dr Johnson's 'last refuge of the scoundrel'. Love of country ('nation') may be desirable and valuable and it is certainly a value that most states want their schools to inculcate. However, how that can be done without setting patriotism and love of country against more negative feelings about other states and other groups within states has so far proved difficult.

The tension between a sense of nation on the one hand and warfare on the other is increased by the ways in which history (discussed in Chapter Four) and geography (discussed in Chapter Two) are taught in schools across Europe. It would appear that all states still use these areas of the curriculum to sustain national myths and maintain a memory of historic victories or wrongs. As will be discussed later in this book, all states teach, to a greater or lesser extent, both founding myths, as Sharma (1991) demonstrates in relation to Holland but also geography which often places an inordinate amount of emphasis on the centrality and innate cohesion of the state.

If anything, issues around the teaching of the language(s) of the state and their complex relation to its history and geography are even more potentially divisive as they move out of the classroom and into a broader and more fiercely contested political arena (discussed in Chapters Three and Four). No state in Europe is monolingual hence nearly all European states have serious problems over language teaching. At times the debates about which languages are to be used and taught in schools threaten the state with violence as will be demonstrated later in the book (exemplified in Chapters Eight, Nine, Ten and Eleven).

All these complex issues argue for greater understanding and sensitivity amongst educational policy makers and teachers. Children and young people might be given a more open view of themselves, their state ('nation') and others. The rest of this book is an attempt to review these issues and to offer ways in which they can be understood.

2 Insiders and Outsiders in European Schooling

New Europe, new borders?

One key educational task is helping pupils and students to locate themselves. In their state, in their global or geo-political region, in the world. Thus the knowledge of boundaries is important, particularly if those boundaries are disputed, as they are still in many parts of Europe. Teaching boundaries in geography or history lessons seems almost a self evident element of the learning of a future citizen. Yet, too often as Noel Malcom notes:

> There is indeed something rather artificial about writing the history of a unit of territory, as a unit, when its defining borders have been a political reality only for the last few decades of that history... there are histories of eighteenth-century Italy, although there was no country called Italy at that time; there are histories of Bulgaria which go back centuries, and there are histories of Greece down the ages, even though the modern borders of Greece were finalised only in 1947 (Malcom, 1998, p. xxxiv).

Contentious and disputed boundaries are not just a post-communist issue, as the examples of Cyprus and Ireland continue to demonstrate. However, it is perhaps most obvious across Eastern Europe where, since the fall of communism, many new states have sprung up, some re-creations, some newly invented, as Table 1 indicates.

Many of these states have disputed borders or at best, borders enforced by international agreement as in the post-Dayton state of Bosnia Herzegovina (Chandler, 2000). This creation or re-creation of new states across Europe after varying degrees of conflict is more than an illustration of the continuing reshaping of the continent by conflict or violence. It also shows that the idea of boundaries, borders, frontiers, marches, however these are defined, is a complex one. This is because all the words imply an ending of authority and power, with those on the inside subject to both and those on the outside free of both or subject to another authority. In either case, those on the other 'side' may be seen as potentially threatening.

Table 2.1. 'New' European states

State	UN	Admitted	Council of Europe	Admitted
Armenia	Yes	1992	No	
Azerbaijan	Yes	1992	No	
Belarus	Yes	1991	No	
Bosnia and Herzegovina	Yes	1992	No	
Croatia	Yes	1992	Yes	1996
Czech Republic	Yes	1993	Yes	1993
Estonia	Yes	1991	Yes	1993
Georgia	Yes	1992	Yes	1999
Kazakhstan	Yes	1992	No	
Latvia	Yes	1991	Yes	1995
Lithuania	Yes	1991	Yes	1993
Moldova	Yes	1992	Yes	1995
Russian Federation	Yes	1991	Yes	1996
Slovakia	Yes	1993	Yes	1993
Slovenia	Yes	1992	Yes	1993
The former Yugoslav Republic of Macedonia	Yes	1993	Yes	1995
Ukraine	Yes	1992	Yes	1995

Sources: Council of Europe, 2000b; United Nations, 2000

In many periods of history, the area between two such authorities has been vague, as terms like the Welsh Marches in the UK indicate. Marches were areas of contestation as indeed were (are) areas called frontier lands and borderlands. As state power consolidated in Europe, through governments succeeding in achieving monopolies over the means of violence, authority in such areas became more definite though rarely as strong as power in more central areas of the state. Authority was still weak in these places and remained so in Europe until well into the 19th century: indeed, such marginal areas still exist in many European states, especially in the Caucasus or the Balkans.

As well as borderlands within Europe, Europe itself, however defined, has its own borderlands, particularly in the East. It is not without significance that a recent popular account of Ukrainian history is called *Borderland* (Reid, 1998). This eastern 'borderland' to Europe is of long origin and is an indication of the constant pressure on European states that has originated from the east, its most recent manifestation being the Ottoman Empire. This pressure was conceived in a Eurocentric way by its being linked to the boundaries of Christendom, so that warfare became not just territorial but religious, the Crusades being perhaps the most obvious example. As a result, Islam has usually been seen as a non-European religion. It is in fact no more non-European than Christianity, it just has been in Europe for a lesser period of time. But the myths remain powerful. The meeting of Islam and Christianity is still regarded asymmetrically. The opponents of the Crusaders remain magnificent barbarians, perhaps best exemplified in Sir Walter Scott's influential novels *The Talisman* and to a lesser extent *Ivanhoe*. Modern historiography paints a rather different picture (Gabrieli, 1969; Irwin, 1997; Maalouf, 1984). They demonstrate how much Christian Europe learned from the Arabs and how many of the so-called European advances in science and technology were in fact based on Arab/Islamic knowledge. As Steven Runciman notes 'our glance must move from the Atlantic to Mongolia' (Runciman, 1965, p. xi). European education has yet to make this change of glance to any significant extent.

To the West of this European borderland, European states developed in competition with one another, competition that was often violent and which frequently focused on the determination of state boundaries. This process continues today. However, boundaries do not just define nation states nor are they simply lines on maps. They are important indicators of inclusion and exclusion and as such, have a range of unclear spatial sites that inscribe children's views of their history and culture as well as their geography. The number of states which incorporate maps or other forms of geographical representation (stars and stripes) on their national flags indicates the importance of boundaries in the establishment of national identities. And maps are not just the clear, precise and simple delineations of boundaries. They are also representations of ideological perceptions of the world (Black, 1997). The Mercator convention commonly used in Europe for wall maps of the world over-emphasises the size of the continent as well as giving it global centrality. A school atlas in Greece stresses Byzantium, one in Serbia the aspirations of a greater Serbia. The layouts are similar, the motherland in the opening pages followed by the rest of the world in descending order of importance (and scale) for that state. Atlases that take a different view have to make this clear in their title as Crow's *Third World Atlas* (Crow, 1983). Children thus learn early on about not just the centrality and importance of their state but also its clear boundaries. In some cases, they also learn boundaries that contain territory lost to other states but still claimed. As Norman Davies notes, '... although most European nations are aware that their present territory was once ruled by foreign powers, dominated by different cultures or inhabited by alien peoples... on the other hand, present day nations and regimes have a strong inclination to believe that they and their forebears have possessed their present territory since time immemorial' (Davies, 1999, p. 39).

The part of the school and university geography curriculum here is important, for as European nationalism grew in the 19th century across Europe so did mass education, which had as one of its roles the duty to ensure that children were (and are) '... thoroughly indoctrinated with the notion that every inch of ground within their national frontiers was eternally "theirs" and hence inherently "French" or "German" or "Polish" or whatever' (Ibid.).

Maps as part of an indoctrination process is not what most cartographers may have had in mind but their products continue to play a role in helping give seeming clarity to concepts of national and international inclusion and exclusion as debates about appropriate map projections demonstrate (Black, 1997; Crosby, 1997). Although young peoples' mental maps may appear to lack the clarity of a printed map, their purpose is similar - to locate the important, to help work out what is 'ours' and what is not 'ours' or is contested.

Insiders and outsiders

Racism and nationalism thrive on the division of the world, at whatever level, into the simple binary grouping of 'them' and 'us', 'our side' and 'their side', insiders and outsiders, ourselves and others, the civilised and the barbarians: all of these categories have the potential to justify the use of state approved violence. Outsiders, 'them', are not only different from insiders, they are potentially dangerous to the insiders, 'us'. But the outsiders help to bind together the insiders. They may form, as Franco Moretti notes 'a hostile Other as the source of collective identity' (Moretti, 1999, p. 29). In the British case, the construction of a British identity from existing English, Scots, Irish and Welsh conflicting identities was a deliberate policy by the English dominated state in response to a range of dangerous 'others'. Linda Colley demonstrates this in her careful analysis of

18th and 19th century British history, showing that Britain, like all other states, was an invented nation:

> ... forged, above all, by war. Time and time again, war with France brought Britons, whether they hailed from Wales or Scotland or England, into confrontation with an obviously hostile Other and encouraged them to define themselves collectively against it. They defined themselves as Protestants struggling for survival against the world's foremost Catholic power. They defined themselves against the French as they imagined them to be, superstitious, militarist, decadent and unfree. And increasingly as the wars went on, they defined themselves in contrast to the colonial peoples they conquered, peoples who were manifestly alien in terms of culture, religion and colour (Colley, 1996. p. 5).

It was this British national identity that was strengthened by two world wars last century and which is now increasingly being eroded as its very foundations disappear. The British no longer share a Protestant oppositional culture in any meaningful sense save for the Ulster-British in Northern Ireland. The French and the Germans are Britain's allies (if not friends) and the once colonial 'Other' is now an integral part of the cities of the UK. Popular hostility to the EU is a pale shadow of the xenophobic fears of the past, although it has the potential to become as xenophobic. Such changes have meant that there is less need of a British identity formed in such an oppositional manner. As a consequence, the national identities that had never really been suppressed have re-emerged in the current nationalist movements towards devolution and independence. One of the key popular aspects of these movements has been in relation to the violent interactions between the states of the United Kingdom. The film *Braveheart*, was a powerful manifestation of these conflicts, portraying the English as evil oppressors of the Scots, which of course they were. However, history teaching across the UK has yet to catch up with such a perspective on English internal colonialism.

Boundary setting is a part of what Anderson has defined as 'imagined communities' (Anderson, 1991). The imagined European state, formed out of war for the most part, sees as part of its sustaining ideology its status as a 'nation', in which all citizens are part of a group with shared values and shared history. State schooling subsequently has as one of its key tasks the inculcation of this sustaining myth. As mass schooling was previously mainly in the hands of the churches, this set the scene for the 19th

century struggle for control of mass education between the churches and the state, a conflict which continues to this day in many European states (Archer, 1979). France provides a classic example of this process of a state disguising itself as a nation and the struggle for control of mass education to support that process (Archer, 1979; Appadurai, 1990; Green, 1991). In the process of state formation, other less powerful nations - Brittany, Catalonia, Provence, Pays Basque, Corsica, Piedmont - were wholly or partially submerged (Braudel, 1989). Though national manifestations of these submerged nations such as flags and cultural events are now more prevalent in the Fifth Republic, with the important exception of Corsica, France is so far avoiding the tendency to fissiparousness displayed by the UK and Spain. Its educational system still resolutely puts forward a firm view of '*la patrie*'. Its borders, however, defined as 'natural' by Danton are actually anything but natural (Doyle, 1989, p. 200). They were defended (and even extended) by the first of the new citizen armies. Indeed the link between a mass citizenry and a mass army of citizens was one of the great inventions of the French Revolution and sustained the mass wars of the 19th and 20th centuries (Keegan, 1997). The process of locating the others against whom 'we' have to be defended continues to this day across Europe, implicitly and explicitly supported by schools and universities.

Europe and its states were and continue to be invented as oppositional concepts, mainly in relation to Christianity's internal divisions (Orthodox, Catholic, Protestant) and also in relation to the struggle with Islam. In the case of Europe as a whole, medieval Christendom and modern Europe to a large extent share common borders and maintain similar sets of insiders and outsiders. This was exemplified by responses to Turkey's application to join the EU. It is further manifest in the anti-Islamic aspects of the violence in Bosnia-Herzegovina, Kosovo and Chechnya. Another hostile 'outsider' presence for western Europeans has frequently been Russia and the USSR. Since Napoleon's defeat in 1812 and the subsequent progress of the Russian army into Paris, fear of Russia has never been far from western capitals. The expansionist policies of the Tsars and of the Soviets met hostile responses in the west from the Crimean War, through support for Japan in 1905, to the Cold War. The break up of the Soviet Union has done little to obviate these fears. The geographically incorrect but politically laden terminology of eastern and western Europe is maintained within the geography curriculum and cultivated ignorance about the Transcaucasus maintains prejudice against both Russians and Islamic groups. Moreover, recent changes in international relations, following the collapse of Communism in Europe, have introduced and/or confirmed ideas concerning insiders and outsiders, based on a division of Europe that has seemingly replaced the old Cold War divide into its replacement, the EU/non-EU divide.

The relationship between school geography and warfare involves not only the question of where the borders are but, more importantly, why they have to be defended with such ferocity. Border change in Europe is a commonplace. It is not an exclusively post-Soviet phenomenon. Within the last hundred years EU states such as France, Germany, Italy and the UK have all changed their borders significantly. One reason for the ferocity, at a continental level, may relate to migration and the struggle for finite resources. This may be one reason why the eastern boundary of Europe remains contested, because of course, it is mainly from the East that people have moved into Europe. Ethnic succession and conflict, as expressed by the Chicago School (e.g. Park, 1967) in relation to cities in the 20th century, is not new but has been a feature of life in the Western Eurasian peninsula for thousands of years (Davis, 1997). Reciprocally it has been to the 'east' that the 'west' has looked for resources from Hitler's *lebensraum* to current conflicts to gain control of the supply of Kazhak oil. Wars between Europe and Russia or Islam have been presented as crusades to save civilisation as 'we' know it. The clash of civilisations legitimates the extreme savagery of these conflicts.

However, if the eastern border of Europe is contested, this state of affairs is seldom reported or investigated in the schools and universities of Europe. This is because conventional definitions have held sway for a long time in our schools. As a UK school atlas of the late 1830s put it:

> According to the decisions of modern science, Europe is bounded on the south by the Mediterranean Sea, on the west by the Atlantic Ocean, which includes the Azores Islands and Iceland; Greenland being considered a part of North America. On the north, its boundary is the Arctic Ocean, comprehending the remote islands of Spitzbergen and Nova Zembla. Towards the east, the limits of Europe seem even yet to be inaccurately defined. Its natural and geographical boundaries might easily be obtained by tracing the river Ousa from its source to its junction with the Belaia, thence along the Kama to the Volga, which would constitute a striking natural division, to the town of Sarapta, whence a short line might be carried due west to the river Don, which would complete the unascertained line of demarcation. But this great outline, through the petty governments under the dominion of Russia, science has

hitherto been prevented from adopting (Russell, c.1838, p. iii.).

Only a modest change of language would make the definition one that many people would accept (and teach) today. For example, in the 1990 *Cambridge Encyclopedia*, Europe is defined as the:

> Second smallest continent, forming an extensive peninsula of the Eurasian land-mass, occupying c. 8% of the Earth's surface, bounded N and NE by the Arctic Ocean, NW and W by the Atlantic Ocean, S by the Mediterranean Sea, and E by Asia beyond the Ural Mts (Crystal, 1990, p. 423).

More, Russell's reference to Russia has contemporary resonance as events in Chechnya, Inguchettia and Georgia reveal. Earlier in this chapter it was suggested that maps, despite their seeming precision, are socially and ideologically constructed. Prose accompanying maps may disguise this but does not completely conceal it. Even the Cambridge Encyclopedia definition does not comment on why other extensive peninsulas of the Eurasian landmass do not merit continental status, for example the Indian sub continent. It also retains unquestioningly the Russell boundaries in broad measure. This is because running alongside such definitions is a widely held value judgement about relative *worth* which still persists, albeit more implicitly and unrecognised now. In this value judgement, those of us lucky enough to live in Europe, however defined, are perceived to have greater moral (and economic and cultural) value than inhabitants of other areas of the globe. To return to Russell:

> This portion of the globe, though least in dimension, is of more importance than any other, not merely to its own inhabitants, but to all who think commerce, science and the arts, of any advantage to mankind. In modern times it has been the seat of literature; and its natives have been justly distinguished for their power, wisdom, courage and strength of intellect: of which, imperishable monuments may be found in the extent of their dominions, the purity of their religion, the principles of their legislation, and the comprehensiveness of their laws (Russell, c. 1838, p. iii).

This reads like a manifesto for European colonisation. It is also a tacit rephrasing of the idea of the barbarians at the gate, a concept that could be said to define Europe and European perspectives on the rest of the world. The creation of the European is also simultaneously the creation of the non-European, the barbarian, the other.

Such a view of insiders and outsiders is more than an abstruse debate about the educational function of cartography and boundaries. It also has within it stereotypes as to who is an insider. If an insider in Europe is a European, what exactly does that term mean and at what point in the curriculum are children given a definition or introduced to the category? The point of the question is that without examination, children and young people are likely to maintain a view of Europeans as white, Christians, a perspective that encourages a view of black Europeans or European Muslims as outsiders. The latter point is particularly relevant in relation to the recent warfare in Bosnia-Herzegovina, Kosovo, Georgia and Chechnya. The gradual integration of the EU countries and the promotion by Brussels of the 'European dimension' in the curriculum could well be leading to a new, international sense of European identity that might replace previous national and nationalist identities. However, there is the danger that this might become a supranational, European supremacist nationalism that is ignorant and denigrating of the widest international context.

These views have their national equivalents. They would hold true for many in England in relation to their own part of the state they live in. It is a view that is nurtured by the mass media and also by the concentration on England rather than the UK as a whole in the National Curriculum for England and Wales. The interesting change in relation to intranational views of insiders and outsiders as a result of new perceptions about boundaries that has occurred recently in the UK appears to be as a result of devolution. What do teachers in English schools teach about the geography of Scotland and Wales, the English's seemingly new 'near abroad'? Asking children in a secondary school recently to write down what they knew about Wales produced very short lists. To ask the same question in a Welsh classroom about England would likely have markedly different result. In other words there is a danger of building a new insider/outsider category unless deliberate efforts are made in schools and universities (and elsewhere) to maintain an inclusive view of Britain. At its worst, it could be compared to the curriculum in Soviet schools in the Baltic States, which was used as a powerful instrument of Russification. When the power relations in the three states were reversed in 1991 Russian language and culture all but disappeared from the curriculum. The large Russian neighbour remains a major trading partner and the land of allegiance for many of the new states' citizens (Coulby, 1997). The Scottish curriculum still teaches children more about England than about their own country. As the Scottish parliament takes firmer control of the curriculum, will this herald the emergence of an (understandable) anti-English curriculum? Certainly there is some evidence of an increase in hostility in schools in England and Scotland to pupils who come from the other nation as part of the pattern of continuing migration within the United Kingdom. Migration and the concept of a unified national citizenry sit uncomfortably together.

Movement and migration

Migration has always been a problem for European states, which is why it is rarely studied in depth in schools. All of the inhabitants of Europe are migrants or are of migrant/refugee descent if one goes back far enough in time. How people become 'indigenous' or autochthonous is not well understood. It is not simply about being born in a state, gaining work and residential permits or even voting rights and citizenship, although all of these are important constituent parts. In the English language we talk of 'second', 'third' and even 'fourth generation immigrants' but only in relation to certain groups of people. Such stigmatised groups are usually not white. In other words, dominant groups determine who is an insider and who is not. And thus is maintained the traditional xenophobic European view of long standing groups of so called 'outsiders' - Jews, Roma and Muslims - who, often as refugees, have frequently fled persecution. To these traditional animosities, new ones have been grafted, focused in particular on groups of relatively recent refugees and other migrants, the product of international in-migration to Europe in the last 50 or so years. Thus, the demographic picture is not so much an objective photograph but a confusing abstract, interpreted according to the prejudices of the observers. In some European states such as Latvia (52%) and Estonia (62%), the dominant populations are barely majorities. A similar situation is to be found in Northern Ireland where just 51% of the population are Protestants, the dominant group.

Again, it is important to note that there is a close link between warfare and migration. The huge movements of people in Europe following the ending of the two world wars and a smaller but similar migration following the end of the Cold War are important events seldom examined in schools. Academic definitions apart, many children see migrants as an alien category, an excluded 'them'. In the case of the UK they have been recently seen as black, to the point that the term 'immigrant' has passed into popular meaning as a black person rather than a migrant who has entered the country. To maintain exclusion over time, terms like 'first generation' and 'third generation' are applied, nearly always to people who are seen as non-white by the dominant white majority, helping to perpetuate exclusion and sustain racism and xenophobia. More recently, migration as fleeing persecution has meant that larger numbers of asylum seekers and refugee children are in schools in the UK. Current government plans for their dispersal across the country mean schools will have these new children without having a clear idea as to why they are there. The potential for exclusion and stigmatisation is high.

The movement of people and its explanation is likely to be covered in geography lessons or not at all. The dynamic of world demography is migration and settlement. It is also a continuing dynamic in Europe that too often is seen as recent, as aberrant and as upsetting an imaginary *status quo*. Yet European classrooms are full of movement and migration that is seldom discussed and even more rarely explained. As an example, London has more languages spoken than anywhere else in the world, with children in schools speaking more than 307 languages, with one third of its 850,000 pupils not speaking English at home (Baker and Eversley, 1999). Similar linguistic variety, albeit on a smaller scale, would be found in many European cities. It is not new and it is continuous. Indeed it has made Europe the complex demographic area that it is today and formed the complex mosaics of people - socio-spatial patterning - that are an outstanding feature of many of Europe's cities.

Socio-spatial patterning

Charles Booth's socio-economic maps of London, with different streets in different colours, from black where what he called the criminal classes lived to the gold of the wealthy, still have a value today. They attempt to visualise the stark, socio-spatial patterning of cities. They are early attempts to delineate social exclusion. The founder of the Chicago School, Park, moved the analysis further, stating 'the processes of segregation establish moral distance which makes the city a mosaic of little worlds which touch but do not interpenetrate' (Park, quoted in Moretti, 1999, p. 89). Both he and Booth make a clear case for moral as well as physical distance between the excluded and the included, a distinction which continues to bedevil much discussion of the subject, best summed up by the phrases 'the deserving' and 'the undeserving poor'. In addition, in the larger cities of western Europe, there is a clear overlap between racial and social stratification. The existence of a differentiated housing market means that this stratification has a clear urban geography. To the extent to which the geography curriculum adopts the vocabulary of deficit with regard to urban segregation - inner city, sink estates, slum housing, problem areas - it is likely to entrench existing prejudices. The geography of poverty is too often perceived as that of social deviance or racial purity.

This is a return to the discussion about boundaries, 'them' and 'us', with which this chapter started. But the focus has come down to inequalities within the state, especially within the city. Walter Benjamin described it perceptively:

> A city is uniform only in appearance. Even its name takes on a different sound in the different neighbourhoods. In no other place - with the exception of dreams - can the phenomenon of the border be experienced in such a pristine state as in cities (Benjamin, quoted in Moretti, 1999, p. 80).

The linguistic richness mentioned earlier in relation to London is echoed by that city's internal boundaries. Areas like Brixton, Green Lanes, Notting Hill, Southall and Tower Hamlets contain specific cultural groups that have many of the characteristics first identified by the Chicago School in terms of territoriality and boundaries. In times of conflict and warfare of course these boundaries are hardened into phenomena such as the Berlin Wall, the Peace Line in Belfast or the Green Line in Nicosia. They may then form the boundaries for migration or ethnic concentration and cleansing. Whilst the history curriculum may be condemned as being overly concerned with warfare, geography might be seen to ignore it. In England and Wales, divided cities, ethnic cleansing and religious hatred are seen as being distant, 'eastern' phenomenon. The social geography of Derry and Belfast are all too easily overlooked.

Thus, seemingly abstract discussions of boundaries and how they are taught about in school are far from being abstract. If otherness can lead to hatred, which it often does, the foundations are laid for violence. In extreme cases it has led to war and will continue to do so. Schools of course cannot stop this process but they can make more determined efforts to help pupils understand them.

3 European Nations, States and Xenophobic Education

Nations and states

At first glance, the EU states' educational aspirations seem wholly laudable. Few people do not wish for economic security and the ending or diminution of social exclusion consequent upon this security being extended to more of the population. But this desire for *economic* security is predicated upon a rarely asked question within most EU education systems, namely that of personal and group *physical* security. It is as if the aims and objectives of 19th century educators have been forgotten, namely that the educational system should provide for the future economic and political success of the state *alongside* its social stability and the social, intellectual and moral development of its citizenry. Clearly, these educational aspirations have contradictory elements, as was indeed recognised in the 19th century when the debates about the purposes of education were being strongly contested (Williams, 1957, 1961). However, these debates seem to have been forgotten in most of the state educational systems of the EU, if not in other European education systems, in recent years. Yet to forget such history or indeed, any history, is a dangerous educational path to take.

Of course, EU education systems do not ignore history, in particular, the history of the state and its relations with other states. The important thing to remember here, however, is that there is not a single state history, accepted by all citizens but that there are many other, perhaps competing histories and these other histories have both educational and political significance. Crimea, Chechnya, Kosovo, Northern Ireland, Pais Vasco and Sardinia are just a few examples of parts of European states whose inhabitants may well not share a common history with that put forward in the state educational system.

All European states are multicultural in that they contain a range of peoples and citizens with differing histories, cultural practices, languages and religions. A case could be further made that just about all UN states are the same. As states have formed over the last millennium, the whole globe has become a complex pattern of states, ranging in size from the vast, like the PRC (China), to the minute, like Fiji and other small island states, which have populations far smaller than say the population of the Crimea or the Isle of Wight (The Times, 1991). A similar pattern is faced in Europe, where large states like Russia sit uncomfortably alongside much smaller states like Estonia.

Moreover, there is no real rationale for the system of states that we live in. A taxonomy would most likely reveal a range of founding circumstances, with colonialism and decolonisation being perhaps the most numerously significant factor. In Europe, the Roman, Byzantine, Holy Roman, Spanish, Austrian and Russian empires have all been important shapers of the state patterning of today. Further afield, Chinese, Japanese, Dutch, German, US and British forms of colonialism have also been significant (Ferro, 1996). However, the formation of states remains an evolving process with boundaries constantly changing, an issue discussed earlier in Chapter Two. It is also worth reiterating that such changes still involve force or the threat of force and that the changes are inevitably reflected in school curricula. In the last century in Europe, such changes have often taken place after internal paroxysms such as those following the wars of 1914-18 and 1939-45. The notion of stable European borders remains a fallacy. The break up of Yugoslavia, the Soviet Union and Czechoslovakia provide a reminder that lines on the European map are constantly being redrawn. France, Germany, Italy and the United Kingdom all changed their boundaries in the last century, in most cases more than once (see Chapter Two).

A key contemporary issue in relation to this book is the *internal* configuration of the state, its stability or otherwise. This is part of the phenomenon behind the decline in war between states but an increase in civil wars within states. According to a recent report from the Stockholm based International Peace Research Institute, there were no inter-state wars but there were 30 internal civil wars in 1995 (Bellamy, 1996). However, by 1997, that figure had gone up to 35, according to the equally respected Humanitarian Law Project (Parker and Heindel, 1997). Although the difficulty of being exact about where civil disorder becomes civil war means exact numbers are always going to be contested, it is likely that a steady increase is currently the trend, including within Europe.

In relation to individual state education systems, this means that while curricula remain nationalist and ethnocentric, they are also concerned with the maintenance of some fictional state unity, best expressed in the oxymoron, the 'nation state'. Many nations/peoples live in more than one state (Albanians, Basques, Catalans, Germans, Hungarians, Greeks, Russians and Turks for example). Most states contain a variety of nations (in Belgium, Dutch, Walloons and Germans). The modern state hardly ever consists of one nation but frequently contains many, although state politicians often find the concept difficult. Perhaps it is a difficulty in the English language itself. Certainly, during the 1997 British General Election campaign, the two contenders for national leadership, Tony Blair and John Major, were cheerfully confused. Blair, a Scot, said:

> I am a patriot. I love Britain and I am proud to be British. I will tell you what being a patriot means to me. It is not about waving a flag. It's about what's in your heart knowing that for a nation to be strong the society must be strong (Jones, 1997, p. 11).

Major, who is English, was equally confused about where a nation stopped and a state took over, saying, in lines reminiscent of the Anglican Creed:

> I believe in one United Kingdom, in one nation and in a Conservative party open to all (Ibid.).

Indeed it is part of state political myth-making to maintain that there is one united nation, worried by external and internal threats to its stability and existence. This myth making is of course not confined to states. The nations that live in such states also manufacture their own myths, their own 'imagined communities' along lines demonstrated by Benedict Anderson (1991). Newly arrived groups may also develop their own myths but these are fiercely contested by existing groups. At a simple level, words like 'foreigner', 'guest worker', 'immigrant' and even 'minority' and their non-English equivalents, frequently carry loaded and negative meanings in school classrooms as much as in the wider society.

Such confusions are part of the crisis of identity that engrosses many modern European states. At one level, this relates to the issue that the very existence of the modern state is increasingly being put into question (Baumann, 1992; Hall, 1992). The emergence of super-national organisations, in Europe obviously the EU, is only one component of this. The progress of national and regional movements is another, in Northern Ireland, Corsica, the Basque country, Northern Italy, Croatia, Chechnya. The power of the large trans-national corporations has also undermined the importance and integrity of decisions taken at the level of the state. The consequences of this for education are still emerging though the more a state's education system attempts to bolster its self-image of contented unity against the facts of demography and culture, the more its legitimacy is eroded amongst sections of the state (Coulby, 1996). At one level, this is part of the ongoing debate about the relationship between the local and the global; in particular the impact of globalisation on the intimate aspects of national cultures (Appadurai, 1990; Held, 1996). A significant policy in relation to these issues is the education provided by states for their citizens' children and the relationship between that education and the informal education provided by the home and community. The more congruence there is between these two sets of educational practice, the more likely is it that there will be harmony within the state; the less congruence, the more likely is there to be a propensity for violence and conflict.

Two aspects of educational provision are crucial in this respect:

- the type of schools the state provides or allows;
- what is taught in them.

In relation to the first, this chapter extends and updates the descriptive framework developed in some of our earlier work (Coulby and Jones, 1995) in which types of differentiation are examined in some detail. In relation to the second, the chapter concentrates on an aspect of the curriculum considered particularly important in relation to the theme of this book, namely the History curriculum.

A critical examination of the ways in which the United Kingdom educational systems differentiate between groups reveals the consequences of such differentiation in terms of conflict. The UK state is not as harmonious as many of its political leaders assert. After three decades of violence, the Northern Ireland peace process is far from assured.

The United Kingdom

The United Kingdom is a complicated state that even its own citizens do not fully understand. Its current boundaries were last redrawn as recently as 1921, when most of Ireland gained independence. The United Kingdom's origins are as an English internal empire, conquest being later legitimated by Acts of Union imposed upon the conquered states: Wales in 1535, Scotland in 1707 and Ireland in 1801. The English, Scots and Welsh see themselves as nations, as do the Irish, although the position in Northern Ireland is more complex. There are also quasi-autonomous islands, the Isle of Man and the Channel Islands. There is a range of languages spoken but nearly all the population speaks English. There are other official languages, Gaelic in Scotland, Welsh in Wales, Manx on the Isle of Man and French on the Channel Islands. Scots as a distinct language from English is also gradually gaining acceptance. These linguistic differences reflect national diversity. The UK also has a wide range of urban diversity. Thus, because of relatively recent international migration patterns, many other languages are spoken, some 300 in London schools for example (Baker, 1999).

Over a relatively short time, say from the middle of the 19th century, a British identity has emerged or been invented, containing within it a wide range of national variation (Cannadine, 1995; Grant and Stringer, 1995). Currently, with a relatively small but increasing nationalist exception, most British people comfortably see themselves as, for example, Welsh and British or Scottish and British. Education has been a major element in this transformation, particularly the domination of the English language throughout the state's education systems and the deliberate exclusion of non-British elements in the curriculum. It is only relatively recently that Welsh and Gaelic have been used as the medium of instruction in parts of Wales and Scotland. This respite for minority languages may have come too late, for as the number of Welsh and Gaelic speakers is rising in both countries due to their educational use and more general increasing status, the numbers actually using these languages as their first language is declining (Grant, 1997).

In terms of educational differentiation, a fascinating thing about the United Kingdom is the enormous variety of educational provision, as the following list indicates.

- *Age* The UK has schools for pupils from 3-5, 5-6, 5-11, 8-11, 9-14, 11-16, 11-18, 14-18, 16-18. The range is great, albeit diminishing as national reforms take hold, and there are few signs of any agreement as to which ages should be in the same school. This causes little comment, either within the system or outside. The differentiation is apparently invisible.
- *Attainment* The debate about selection on academic performance or perceived ability is a furious one in the UK but only at the second level of schooling, from the age of 11. It is accepted that there will be change according to the prevailing governmental orthodoxy. The swings in educational fashion here appear to be on a twenty year cycle, recent cycles starting around 1945 with the tripartite system, 1965 with the attempt to introduce comprehensivisation and 1985 with the introduction of new forms of differentiation.
- *Attendance* Nearly all state funded schools are day schools. Many private schools and some segregated special schools (below) are boarding schools. Another apparently invisible differentiation.

- *Behaviour* There are segregated special schools for so-called emotionally and behaviourally disturbed children. Other children may be sent on this basis to special units that may be on or off the sites of mainstream schools and which may be full or part time. Such debate as there is on this is as to where the behavioural cut off point should be made. This debate has both ideological and financial aspects (Daniels and Garner, 1999). However, a current concern is that most of the students in these special schools and units are male and a disproportionate number are black. This fact is used as evidence that the schooling system is failing the black community. An important and contentious issue for some groups.

- *Citizenship* All children resident in the state, including non-citizens, are entitled to free education from age 5-16. It is also compulsory for all parents to ensure their children have an education. Small numbers of parents educate their children at home - a slowly increasing group. Another invisible differentiation.

- *Contact* At school, all teaching is still conventional teacher-pupil interaction. ICT is a small but growing area. It is not yet an aspect of differentiation though political concern has turned to the difference between those children who have networked personal computers at home and those who do not (digital deficit).

- *Curricula* There are separate curricula in each nation of the United Kingdom, England, Wales, Scotland and Northern Ireland. Only England and Wales have the rigidly structured and specified National Curriculum. That of Wales is distinct, however, from England in, for example, history, as well as in the prominence it gives to the Welsh language. Private schools (below) are exempt from the National Curriculum. The variations between the national systems have not yet become a matter of political concern, although that is likely to change as devolution increases.

- *Disability/special educational need* There are separate schools for students perceived to have disabilities, physical and/or mental. This provision can be part or full time; it can be day school or residential. There is a growing trend in favour of integrated, 'inclusive' schooling (Department for Education and Employment, 1997a).

- *Gender* Separate schools for girls and boys are popular in the UK. In particular, many parents prefer separate provision for girls after the age of about 11, often on religious/cultural grounds. This is apparently not a particularly contentious issue for the majority of the population but it is important to certain minorities, especially Muslims.

- *Language* Separate schools for different language groups are a feature of schools in Wales and to a lesser extent Scotland. This is a subject of immense political importance in Wales and potentially so in Scotland and Northern Ireland. In urban areas children for whom English is a second or foreign language are taken out of some lessons for additional support. However, unlike in Germany, there is not a system that separates such children into distinct schools. Little provision is made for maintaining mother tongues other than English, save for Welsh in Wales and Gallic in Scotland.

- *Location* Rural schools are frequently under threat of closure as they are seen as uneconomic. Local people protest but lack political power to stop the process. The innovations and increased pattern of diversity associated with Educational Action Zones (Department for Education and Employment, 1997b) are almost exclusively confined to urban areas.

- *Nationality* Each of the territorial nations in the UK has their own systems. Scotland, in particular, has always had a distinctive system at both school and university. The position in Northern Ireland is more problematic and is referred to throughout this volume.

- *'Race'* De facto segregation, on the basis of residence and parental choice, is accepted, particularly in certain urban areas in England. This is not a major issue for the majority white population, where racism is relatively commonplace and its 'milder' forms socially accepted or invisible. It clearly is an issue for the minority black populations and to a lesser extent for educational and social policy makers.

- *Religion* Separate schools for different religions/denominations, funded by the state, are a feature of the UK system. This is a major issue in Northern Ireland where religion plays a significant part in sectarian hatred (Byrne, 1998). Attempts there to create unified schools have met with little popular support. In the rest of the UK important issues concern which religions the state is prepared to fund to establish schools. The previous monopoly of Catholic, Protestant and Jewish groups is currently being broken with the funding of more Islamic schools and also some for Greek Orthodox, Adventist and Sikh children (Smithers, 1999; Rafferty, 1998; Hackett, 1998; Lepkowska, 1998).

- *Statutory/non-statutory* As well as the formal statutory provision, whether in private or state schools, there are also supplementary (out of school hours) schools. A feature of most EU cities, they are small schools or classes set up by minority groups to do one or more of three things, to teach the community's religion, to supplement what is seen as an ineffective state provision and the teaching of the group's language, cultural history and identity. They are a significant phenomenon with more than a thousand operating in London for example.

- *State monopoly* This is not an issue in the UK system, as it is in many East European systems. After school classes (see above) and private schools (see below) both thrive in the UK system These schools receive little or no state funding but are not seen by many as divisive.

- *Teachers* There are differences between types of teacher in terms of training and status. Teachers in private schools (below) often have no formal training. Teachers are on national pay scales, which differ little between the various national systems. The introduction of differentiated pay scales for teachers (Department for Education and Employment, 1998) will almost certainly increase the importance of this difference.

- *Wealth* Separate schools for the wealthy are a traditional feature of the UK system. The rich and powerful do not send their children to state schools. There are at least two major consequences of this. Firstly, for political decision makers at the state level (New Labour as well as Conservative) the state education system is frequently seen as being for 'other people's' children. Inevitably there is less commitment to ensuring the state system's adequate funding and reform than there would be were all children to utilise it. Secondly, this separate system of well-founded schools with ready access to elite university places serves to reproduce social and economic stratification. Language, culture, ethnic identity and gender are of course all elements in the distinctiveness of these schools and in the resultant stratification.

Obviously the categories within this list may overlap: there are Catholic, residential schools for secondary girls and so on. What this list shows is that much of the differentiation within the system is seen as relatively unproblematic. The areas of disagreement are however, interesting and demonstrate that, even in a relatively stable state, the education system is a potential source and supporter of conflict. In Northern Ireland, the education system is seen as doing little to diminish inter-communal conflict as the two communities continue to be educated in separate schools on the basis of religion. Attempts to unify the system gain little support from either community although the UK government is in favour of integration. Throughout the rest of the UK, religion in education has lost much of its former violently divisive aspect, although there are elements who would have it otherwise. The recent homophobic outbursts from Scottish church leaders in response to proposals for a less stigmatising sex education indicate the potential that religions still have for educational conflict.

The history curriculum and stability within states

In terms of the History curriculum, there are significant differences. In Northern Ireland, the History curriculum in the state funded Catholic schools, although ostensibly the same as in the state funded schools which the Protestant community use, is in practice very different. Indeed, coming to terms with its history is an issue for the whole of Ireland, as the recent flurry of revisionist historiography demonstrates (Hickman, 1996; Kennedy, 1996; Boyce, 1996; Hempton, 1996). However, following devolution, national histories are now emphasised in all the systems in the UK. It is certainly much less the case than it was only a few years ago that Scotland was a country that learned more about another nation's history than it did about its own (Grant, 1997; 1999). The major difference between them is that the schools in England do tend to conflate English history with British history, which perhaps reinforces the general English insensitivity to the differences found within the broader British society. Also, few pupils in English schools are exposed to the less presentable aspects of England's internal colonialism, such as the Troubles in Ireland or the Highland clearances. The exploration of such histories remains arcane. Few students from these communities learned in the past about their own history. Revealing evidence for this is the increasing difficulty in Scottish universities in recruiting faculty members in relation to Scottish history.

All this is demonstrative of confusion about state history and its place within the curriculum of schools. A recent example of such confusion has been the debate in the English education system about the cultural responsibilities of schools having as they do, a culturally diverse student body. Dr Nicholas Tate, former head of the UK government's Schools Curriculum and Assessment Authority for England (SCAA), in arguing for a stronger sense of British identity to be inculcated by the schools, wants a return to an Arnoldian 'best that is known and thought' high culture. He insists that 'the curriculum needs to be firmly and proudly rooted in a cultural heritage with its roots in Greece and Rome, in Christianity and in European civilisation' (Tate, 1996, p. 18). Other traditions are recognised but not as 'British' and consequently in a subordinate and unclear place within the curriculum of state schools in England. It is also revealing that Dr Tate tends to conflate British and English, much to the annoyance of

Scots, Welsh and other British citizens who do not see themselves as English.

Tate's viewpoint or locally configured variations on it could well be accepted by certain powerful conservative or nationalistic educational groups in most state educational systems. In its European manifestations, the key elements are a belief in a common European heritage based on Greek and Roman culture and Christianity. Indeed, lack of such a heritage is a common nationalistic insult in Europe, especially during wars. As Mrs Humphry Ward wrote to former President Roosevelt in 1917, the Germans were true barbarians because '... for all their science and their organisation, they have nothing really in common with the Graeco-Latin and Christian civilisation on which this old Europe is based' (Ward, 1917, p. 165). Similar views of Muslims in former Yugoslavia were expressed by both Serbs and Croatians during the Yugoslavian collapse (Sells, 1996). Indeed, they are still being expressed, as one of the authors of this book discovered during recent (2000) fieldwork in Bosnia-Herzegovina. To make matters more complicated still, as Chapter Two demonstrated, there is no objective agreement on where the boundaries of Europe actually are and who actually is a European. In addition, such a view of a benevolent European civilisation must bear in mind Gandhi's view. When asked what he thought of Western civilisation, he replied that he thought that it would be a good idea. Tate's views reveal the extent to which the discourse on knowledge in the UK is inscribed with European triumphalism. This triumphalism is based on a fallacious and fundamentally racist version of European history (Coulby, 2000a; Zambeta, 2000) prevalent among traditionalists like Tate and in the Europeanising of the EU's education policy.

There are at least three histories that a child learns. The more congruent they are, the more integrated will be the outcome. Hidden or denied histories may well hide hidden hatreds that can burst forth with disastrous consequences. A school history that ignores such community or family (the two do not always coincide) histories is likely to cause more harm than good. Such has been the case in Northern Ireland but there are many other examples across Europe, most notably in former Yugoslavia (Pesic, 1994). What is needed here is the acknowledgement that the gaps may exist and their exploration within the official school history curriculum is a necessity. A dominant history, the official history taught in school, which does not impinge upon the histories of the other two, is in danger of maintaining fears already extant and even exacerbating them. However, if a deliberate effort is made to bring at least some of these histories into contact, a new broader based history may emerge, which all parties to the curriculum can engage with. Nowhere is this more vital than in Northern Ireland but a similar case could be made in relation to the history taught in many schooling systems in Europe. However, history, like any other curriculum area, is not merely a list of content. It is also the intellectual tools that children are given to make sense of what they are learning. The tools for analysis, assessment and judgement can be taught.

What does the UK example demonstrate? First, that all states have difficulties over education and minorities, with the real possibility that education ends up sustaining violent attitudes and behaviour rather than suppressing and opposing it. Second, that political powerlessness, compared to other communities within the state, exacerbates inter-communal conflict, as the poor political position of Catholics in Northern Ireland exemplifies. Third, even if a schooling system succeeds, lack of economic opportunity, particularly if that lack is based upon xenophobia or racism, will slowly diminish the potentially benevolent impact of schooling, a feature found both in Northern Ireland in relation to the Catholic community and in England also, particularly in relation to its African Caribbean black community (Gillborn and Gipps, 1996). Schooling is seen as having no value and teachers' contrary views have little impact compared to the peer group pressure the students face. Fourth, if there is racism, xenophobia and narrow nationalism in the wider society, schools face a difficult task if they wish to combat this, particularly in relation to the dominant white group within UK society. The fifth point is the fact that the UK is a society that has evolved continuously in relation to its diversity over the last few hundred years and that the education system has taken a leading role in this.

What this chapter has attempted to demonstrate so far is that the modern state has a real dilemma in relation to providing an appropriate education for all its citizens' children and young people. If it ignores a group's demands for forms of education that meet with its aspirations, it runs the risk of alienation of that group from the mainstream of state activity. If it meets a group's aspirations, that may in itself help destabilise the state. The state has to examine carefully the forms of education it provides for its citizens' children and young people and the relationship of that educational provision to the informal education given by the home and community. If they differ greatly, there is likely to be discontent or even rejection of the state's provision, with subsequent support for more overt forms of opposition.

A key to much of this is the teaching of history and the state's history curriculum. As has just been mentioned, there are at least three histories that a child learns. Hidden or denied histories hide hatreds which can burst forth with disastrous consequences. This is not to argue for a content free or content crammed history, much more that state history has to teach skills of historical enquiry and judgement with a wider range of examples than is currently the case. A little detail may make the issue clearer. The state history will have the oppositional or 'other' religion(s) but the community history may be the mirror image of this: Catholic against Protestantism or Islam against Christianity for example. In a specific household within a community, a further differing religious perspective may exist as well, perhaps a sectarian split. The state history may well teach about traditional state enemies, the countries with which the state has been at war or had a long rivalry. But for many children in schools in Europe, the state enemy may be the state itself or some state far away across the world. A Macedonian example helps demonstrate this. In his First World War novel, the Greek writer Statis Myrivilis writes of a Macedonian mother his hero meets in the war zone, talking of her sons being dragged off to war:

> First the Serbs took them. They dragged them out of our cart, beat them, and stole them away from me. "You are Serbs", they shouted. "Why don't you want to fight the Bulgarians?" Next came the Bulgarians, together with the Germans. These shouted "You are Bulgarians, forward march to fight the Serbs." And all over again from the beginning: beatings, prison (Myrivilis, 1987, p. 183).

In the face of such family histories, what can schools do? The aim should constantly be the increase in the size of the overlap between the competing histories that exist within the state or, if that proves impossible, to explore the differences more openly. Given all this, it is not surprising that the forces for fissure within the states of Europe are as likely to increase as to decline. Traditionally, warfare united the state, but between states warfare is now increasingly rare. Internal wars are increasing and will in turn enhance the nationalistic feelings of the various warring parties. Again, the example of former Yugoslavia is instructive, with new histories being written and taught, even in newly labelled languages (e.g. Bosnian).

All this appears to indicate is that multinational states are probably inherently unstable and that schools have an all but impossible mission to counter this. In addition, males, the dominant group in all states, may have a propensity for violence, both as young people in schools and as adults in the wider society, although the scientific debate on this is still far from clear (Keegan, 1993). It has frequently been a lethal combination in the literal sense of that word. Yet such states constantly seek to be more stable, using education as a major ideological force for unity and the armed forces as a restorer of unity of last resort. The relationship between education and violence is thus an intimate one.

The state's desire is for unity and the absence of conflict. But a unity forcibly imposed is a false unity, existing only in the minds of the dominant group within a particular state. Education is crucial here. It gives young people the intellectual tools to assess and judge, as well as the material knowledge against which to check and test that communal knowledge that they bring to school (Hewitt, 1996). As important, the less differentiation there is in the system, in contrast to the description of the UK above, the more likely is the success of the integrative power of education. To learn alongside people who are different from oneself, - different in terms of gender, of performance level, in income level, of language or of religion, is the beginning of tolerance and understanding.

4 Knowledge and Warfare

Introduction

To say that Europe invented warfare and that warfare was its principal bequest to the rest of humanity would be an exaggeration but not a large one (Anderson, 1988; Best, 1998; Kiernan, 1998). Since the emergence and consolidation of European nation states from the medieval period onwards, warfare, both against their own populations and against the armies and navies of neighbouring states, has been a characteristic of their history. The period of imperialism spread this systematic engagement in war and conquest, along with its associated European military technology, to the rest of the world. The 20th century in Europe was one of apparently unceasing warfare. Twice in that century, Europe dragged the world into its internecine wars (Mazower, 1998). The progress of the *Wermacht* from Berlin to Stalingrad and back in the company of the Red Army marks one of the most murderous, inhuman and destructive episode in human history (Overy, 1998). It is against such episodes and such a history that Europe's claim to be the birthplace and repository of civilisation must be tested.

In Chapter Three it was argued that there was a tension between the heterogeneous nature of the populations of European states and the state-controlled homogeneity of the content of their school and university curricula. This chapter takes the argument further. It is the contention of this chapter that there is a link between what is taught in schools and universities in particular states of Europe and the potential of those states to embark upon violence. By this is meant an increased likelihood of such states pursuing policies of warfare either with regard to their own populations (internal) or the populations of other states (external). Of course, the curricula of schools and universities are also capable of reducing the propensity of a state to engage in warfare and most EU states would claim that this was so in their own system.

This chapter therefore examines those curricular components that are particularly involved in the processes which implicitly or sometimes explicitly support state (and sometimes personal) violence:

- language policies;
- history and cultural studies;
- religious education;

- scientific research and development programmes;
- military training;
- training in conformity.

In doing so it revisits or prefigures, from a pointedly different angle, some of the themes that are developed in other chapters of this book. This exploration of the links between knowledge and warfare allows the dissonance between demographic heterogeneity and state controlled or approved curricular systems to be heard in its most clear form. And it is this dissonance which has the potential to sustain warfare in many of its potential and actual forms.

Much of this chapter thus makes links between curriculum content and the encouragement of nationalism, xenophobia and racism, basic building blocks of violence. Ignatieff writes:

> It was in Vukovar that I began to see how nationalism works as a moral vocabulary of self-exoneration. No one is responsible for anything but the other side. In the moral universe of pure nationalist delusion, all action is compelled by tragic necessity. Towns must be destroyed in order to liberate them. Hostages must be shot. Massacres must be undertaken. ... Everyone in a nationalist war speaks in the language of fate, compulsion and moral abdication (Ignatieff, 1994, p. 32).

This vocabulary is learned, among other places, in the schools and universities of Europe.

Foreign and first language policies

In relation to language, schools and universities in Europe frequently fail to reflect the linguistic diversity of their state in ways that might have facilitated communication, understanding and tolerance between groups. Even in relation to second language learning, they frequently prefer to adopt a perceived international language such as English as their chosen second language rather than an often 'hidden' internal language. Concentrating on such national linguistic diversity, Greece provides a useful example. The historical background here is complex. Relations with Turkey are a key element - the bad feelings over the population exchange of 1923 following the Treaty of Lausanne and the continuing long term bad political relations over issues such as Cyprus and the Aegean Islands ensure the continuation of a potential for conflict. Other destabilising factors include opposition to the formation of the state of Macedonia (FYROM) and concern over wider Balkan hostilities. Greece has long claimed that its treatment of its Turkish minority (which it continues to refer to as Muslim rather than Turkish), living largely in Thrace, ought to be the example followed by Turkey in the treatment of its parallel Greek minority. Certainly in Thrace there are no official restrictions on the use of Turkish either in schools or in mosques. The educational treatment of Slav speakers, Albanians and Vlachs, elsewhere in Greece, is less positive. To take the latter example, Pettifer reports that officially, as there are no recognised ethnic minorities in Greece, Vlach is not today used in schools, although before the war there were many Romanian-sponsored schools in the Pindus villages. Consequently many Vlachs feel that, as they have never done anything to destabilise the Greek political system, in terms of separatist or nationalist ambitions, they should have more educational recognition of their language. Although a small group whose linguistic distinctiveness may be denied by their neighbours and by the state, the Vlachs retain a strong sense of identity (Pettifer, 1994).

A further example was the behaviour of Cambridge University Press in 1996. An ethnographic study of villages in Northern Greece by Anastasia Karakasidou *Fields of Wheat, Hills of Blood*, was not published by the press for fear of terrorist attacks on CUP and Cambridge University academics working in Greece. The unpublished study showed that the people in the field work considered themselves Macedonian and spoke a Slavonic language, contrary to official Greek claims (Young, 1996). As well as this contested autochthonous national diversity, Greece also has considerable urban diversity such as the relatively recent but numerically significant Polish population in Athens. Often illegal immigrants and without citizenship, the linguistic position of such minorities are even weaker than those of the Vlachs and other autochthonous minorities (Lazardis, 1996; Romaniszyn, 1996).

The results of such a language policy in Greece means that in Thrace children may be taught Turkish but the other minority languages of Greece - Albanian, Vlach, Macedonian - are invisible in schools and universities. The idea that Greek-speaking children should be taught Turkish as a foreign language rather than English would be seen in Athens as academically and politically unthinkable. The language policy of the schools and universities thus reflects the domestic and foreign policy of the state. This policy is not without belligerence. The state wishes Greece to be Hellenocentric with other national identities within the state not to be encouraged. The state is at odds with its Balkan neighbours (except Orthodox Serbia) and context, preferring through its membership of the European Union and NATO to contextualise itself within a European and western set of relations (see, for example the essays in Constas, 1995 and Allison, 1997). At the least, this language policy does nothing to inhibit or reduce political tensions in the eastern Mediterranean.

Latvia provides an example of a state in educational language transition. (This issue is discussed in greater detail in Chapter Nine.) Not surprisingly, Russian was abandoned as a foreign language in Latvian speaking schools soon after independence. Furthermore, the Russian-speaking schools, and especially universities, are rapidly being transformed so that Latvian is the language of instruction. The state has gone through a process of reversed linguistic asymmetry: Russian was in a dominant position and Latvian subordinate in education and society under the former Soviet Union: following independence Latvian is now in a dominant position and Russian in a subordinate. In the Latvian-speaking institutions, the first foreign language, formerly Russian, is now English. There are economic reasons for this as Latvia struggles, with some success, to enter the international economic order. But the change in educational policy is also motivated by political and cultural considerations, as the language of Soviet imperialism is cast off and the language of the (implied free and democratic) west adopted. Unfortunately, however, almost half the population of Latvia is Russian-speaking. Furthermore, Russia itself is a neighbouring state and important, albeit declining, trading partner. The language policy of the Latvian education system is likely to restrict communication both between citizens of the state and with those of its largest and most powerful neighbour. Combined with citizenship laws that made it very difficult for Russian speakers to obtain passports and voting rights, this policy exacerbates political tension between Russia and Latvia. From Moscow, the perception is all too easily that of Russian people and their language being oppressed by a state which also blocks their access to the Baltic Sea and the rich port of Riga. The 1998 Referendum which approved citizenship rights for Russian speakers perhaps presages a less belligerent curricular policy.

The actual linguistic diversity of European states is, as was demonstrated in Chapter Three, an exceedingly complex pattern. It represents a source of cultural and economic capital available to these states. In the spread of global languages, Russian up to 1991 and still English and Chinese, these cultural resources are increasingly at risk. This risk is exacerbated by those school and university curricular policies that enforce the learning of global languages and neglect those of the state's nations and cities. Furthermore, a language is not only a mode of communication, it also embodies and represents a culture. To have access to one's neighbours' languages is to be able to better understand something of their religion, literature, philosophy, laws and way of life more generally.

Another important aspect of language teaching is that in the first language and literature curriculum, the teaching of a set canon of texts remains a feature at school and university in almost all states of Europe. In some countries this canon is well established and authenticated. In countries which have recently emerged or re-emerged, the establishment of the national literary canon is an important element in state building, as is shown with the case of Latvia in Chapter Nine. These canons tend to be national in their structure and nationalistic in their content. They identify rich cultural traditions and achievements with the geography of a particular state. They neglect the literature of other nations within the state, Scottish, say, or Welsh. They make no attempt to encompass the urban diversity that now characterises the populations of so many European states. The actual texts within the canons are not without xenophobia and chauvinism. Indeed actual warfare is all too often a characteristic of the canonical texts: *The Iliad*, the Icelandic, Norse and German sagas, *The Song of Roland*, *Orlando Furioso*, *Henry V*, *The Lusiad*, *the Poem of the Cid*, *Le Rouge et le Noir*, *War and Peace*.

> Come the three corners of the world in arms,
> And we shall shock them! Naught shall make us rue
> If England to itself do rest but true!
> (Shakespeare, *King John*, V, pp. vii, 116-118).

The Mountain Wreath is a 19ᵗʰ century Serbian epic poem about the defeat of the Serbian army at the Battle of Kosovo in 1389. With other epics on the same defeat it has helped to make the Battle of Kosovo an integral part of the national cultural heritage: 'In all European history it is impossible to find any comparison with the effect of Kosovo on the Serbian national psyche' (Judah, 1997, p. 30). The poems and the mythologised version of history together are used within and outside educational institutions to reproduce a highly nationalistic consciousness: or, as Judah concludes, after his analysis of the Croatian and Bosnian wars, 'Serbian history was misused to do harm to others and give power to the few' (p. 310).

Cultural products are themselves closely linked to warfare both as cause and effect. They provide the patriotic and jingoistic rhetoric that helps prepare populations for war. They display warfare in terms of glory, national expansion or survival, heroic individualism and self-sacrifice rather than as plain greed and carnage. Schools and universities are one of the main institutions through which this link between culture and warfare is mediated and reproduced.

History and cultural studies

Turning to history, Greece can again be used as an example. Considering the image of Europe presented in the compulsory textbooks of Greek elementary schools, Flouris discovered that the references 'do not portray the image of Europe conceived by the EU member states. On the contrary, students are exposed to the concept of Europe via wars, conflict etc' (Flouris, 1995, p. 115). Similarly looking at social studies set books across the levels of secondary schooling he discovered that, contrary to the stated aims of the teaching of history in Law 1566-85, young people in Greece become acquainted with other countries via the teaching of wars (Flouris, 1996). The teaching of Hellenic history in Greek schools tends towards the formation of nationalism since it lacks cosmopolitanism and there are no references to other ancient civilisations except the Roman (Massialas, 1995). This centralised curriculum, with its state-endorsed, compulsory textbooks, follows values which are also espoused by a largely traditionalist teaching force. Since it is the other Balkan countries in particular which are presented in the context of war and invasion, during the Byzantine period and the war for independence (Massialas and Flouris, 1994), then the question of the relationship between the compulsory school curriculum and the policy of the state, with regard both to its non-Greek citizens and its Balkan and Mediterranean neighbours, is again one which falls to be addressed. Whilst it might be going too far to suggest that this curriculum stimulates hostility and warfare, it certainly does remarkably little to encourage reconciliation and peace. Identities inscribed with this level of nationalism and xenophobia are a necessary, if not sufficient, condition for warfare.

The discussion in Chapter Three suggested that modern states have tried, with varying degrees of success, to identify themselves with nations. By a process of religious and linguistic intolerance across many centuries the state of France has almost succeeded in disguising itself as the nation of France (Braudel, 1989). In other cases an artificial national identity has had to be manufactured: the United Kingdom has been less successful at persuading the English, let alone the Scots, the Welsh and the Irish, that they are *British* (Grant, 1994; Grant, 1997). Similar difficulties face the governments of Spain, Belgium, Italy and Romania. The national tensions in these countries are strong and enduring. Other states have broken beneath these tensions: the Soviet Union, Yugoslavia, Czechoslovakia, indeed as recently as the early

1920s, the United Kingdom. To return to the example of Greece, the attempt there is to identify the modern state, via Byzantine Orthodoxy, with the city-states of the fourth century BC and thus with Hellenic civilisation (Psomiades and Thomadaki, 1993; Zambeta, 2000). Expansionary policies in the past and belligerent postures in the present are legitimated inside a knowledge system which sees the idealised Greeks as the cradle and repository of European civilisation and which focuses on neighbouring states only in the context of warfare. In attempting to bury the state's recent history of internal and external warfare and conflict beneath a homogenous Greek and Orthodox identity, the curriculum only exacerbates tensions with internal minorities and bordering states. Whilst the educational reform in Greece, implemented in 1998 (Law 2525/1997) explicitly addresses the curriculum and assessment of the *enieo lykeio* (Zambeta, 1999), it does nothing to address its xenophobic content.

The history curricula of schools and universities are ethnocentric in two parallel ways. Firstly, they concentrate on the triumphant emergence of, or ascent to world power of, a particular state. Thus the Golden Century is central in the Netherlands, the Risorgimento in Italy, the industrial revolution and imperial period in England and Wales. Despite aspirations towards European studies or world history, the overwhelming concentration in history teaching in most European states is on national events. (Norway provides a welcome exception here (The Royal Ministry of Education, 1997)). Regional histories, that is those of other nations than that with which the state seeks to confuse itself, are forgotten or deliberately hidden in such systems. The history of Scotland remains concealed from pupils in the schools of England and Wales and indeed, until very recently, from those in Scotland itself. Only by permitting manifold versions of the school history curriculum, has Spain come close to reconciling the intensely felt national passions through which its many histories are codified (Mackey, 1997). Equally lost in such curricular systems are globally important events which took place beyond the state's boundaries: the Spanish invasion of Latin America or the Thirty Years War are neglected topics in the National Curriculum of England and Wales, as the rise and fall of the Japanese Shogunate is across Europe.

The second way in which school and university history curricula are ethnocentric is in their tendency towards overt nationalism. They place undue importance on events, personalities, discoveries, processes and achievements local to one state. They exaggerate the importance of one state in the history of the world.

The history curriculum necessarily pays explicit attention to the subject of warfare. As in all curricular areas there are choices to be made here. Should history be social and economic as well as political? How are the lives of women to be regarded in school and university history? The decision to teach political and military history is likely to mean that other forms and versions of history are marginalised. Once military history has become central, the influence of the state is certain to be all the more firmly felt. The former Yugoslav school curriculum taught of the defeat and exploitation of Serbia not only by Turkey but also by other constituent nations of the state (Rosandic and Presic, 1994). It taught of the world's indifference to Serbia's suffering. (To point this out is by no means to deny the magnitude of this suffering (Judah, 1997)). It encouraged hatred for other groups in the state and disdain for international opinion. In times of war, or in near war conditions, this tendency in the history curriculum may be exacerbated. In primary schools in the southern part of Cyprus there is a subject called, 'I learn, I don't forget and I fight for the freedom of my country'. Whilst at one level this is absolutely understandable, at another it gives a stark example of an uninhibited relationship between curriculum and warfare.

Of course to ignore conflict and warfare in history can be as much of a political message as to concentrate on it. In the United States the history of the slave trade and slavery is receiving grudging acknowledgement in schools and universities, but the genocide of the Plains Indians is a matter which is still largely ignored (Lamawaima, 1995). The history curriculum at school and university in Germany and the United Kingdom is faced with similar dilemmas. To what extent should children and young people in the United Kingdom learn about the English conquest and subjugation of Wales, Scotland and Ireland, the slave trade and its importance in the generation of the wealth which fuelled the industrial revolution, or the treatment of native people in Australia? In what ways can young people in Germany be exposed to the history of the holocaust (Supple, 1993) and of the nature of the Second World War on the Eastern Front? That the curricular systems in both states largely shy away from these matters betrays the tendency to hide and deny these components of their history rather than a decision to concentrate on other aspects of historical studies or on more peaceful epochs.

Religious education

Religious education remains in many countries a cornerstone of xenophobia. Again the links between religion and warfare are manifold and school and university curricula are only one of the instruments of their mediation and reformulation. In Northern Ireland and in Cyprus, as well as in the former Yugoslavia, religion remains one of the major fuses for actual conflict. Nor is this link maintained only within the subject of religious education. Even in those states, such as France, where education is secular, the history and literary presentations of crusades and *jihads* assist in the maintenance of the link between religion and warfare.

The survival of religious institutions and curricula in so many states in Europe and elsewhere is one of the triumphs of traditionalism over the Enlightenment project. These traditionalist survivals are all the more remarkable in that they occur in societies that are overwhelmingly secular. It is widely believed that, during the 19th century, in states such as the United Kingdom and France the state gradually took responsibility for education away from the churches (Archer, 1979). In the case of the United Kingdom, the Netherlands or Belgium this underestimates the extent to which the churches were able to infiltrate the emerging state control of education and retain a strong traditionalist presence.

This strong part played by religious authorities in many states reinforces and reproduces one strand of pluralism whilst ignoring and denigrating another. In the Netherlands, Catholic and Protestant groups are able to administer both schools and polytechnics. Educational institutions provide a site where these cultures and practices can focus, develop and reproduce. On the other hand this strength is frequently denied to other groups, though Muslim groups have now succeeded in establishing their own schools (Dwyer and Meyer, 1995). In the United Kingdom Catholic, Protestant and Jewish groups have all been able to obtain substantial state financial backing for their primary and secondary schools for many years. However, only recently, with the coming to power of New Labour, have a few Islamic school succeeded in obtaining such backing (Lepkowska, 1998). The idea that the compulsory daily act of worship in England and Wales should be Islamic would be anathema to policy makers even with reference to those schools in London where every child is a Muslim. Though some rights of religious recognition have been achieved in those schools which have a predominantly Islamic population (Sarwar, 1993), a secular, multi-faith approach is the best that can be tolerated, with rare exceptions even in religiously diverse urban areas. The secular curriculum and ethos of the state schools of France continues to come into conflict with those Islamic pupils and students who wear traditional religious costume to school. All such examples confirm the ambiguities about Islam that most European states continue to maintain, almost a Crusade by other means.

Control of educational institutions by religious authorities and religious education as an aspect of the school curriculum have rarely been elements of European education systems which have served to increase tolerance and respect for plurality. Rather, they have served to allow particular cultural groups to maintain an undue influence over education, often at the expense of other, less powerful groups. The Greek Orthodox Church continues to use schools and teachers in its active campaigns against what it considers to be heresy (Karaflogka, 1997). Religious intolerance is one of the capacities which facilitates the waging of war. In Chechnya and Tibet, on the other hand, it is secularised education in schools that is one of the ways in which war is conducted by other means.

Whilst the importance of traditionalism is appropriately being stressed, there is an aspect to the survival of religious elements inside education systems which is a component of modernity. In most cases the religion favoured in schools and universities is that favoured by the state itself: Orthodox in Greece, Catholic in Ireland, Protestant in Norway, generically Christian in England and Wales, secular in France. These religions are not only those that obtain arbitrary state approval, they are those of either a majority of the population or of its most powerful groups. Furthermore, they are part of the legitimation in which the state presents itself. Education is only one of the policies whereby the state legitimates itself through performing in ostensibly religious (or secular) ways. Others include those on contraception, abortion, divorce, blasphemy and, less overtly, immigration. Thus the teaching or practice of religion in European schools and universities also provides instruction to children and young people on the nature of the state to which they belong. Even in countries such as England where religion has long since ceased to be an important component either in society or in the identities of the bulk of the population, religious education and worship in schools teaches children that the state ('the nation', 'the culture', 'the people') is Christian. Whilst part of the intended function of this is doubtless to engender an enhanced sense of social solidarity and cohesiveness, it is actually selective with regard to the religion it endorses, even within the strange category of generic Christianity, and is thereby socially divisive. If the state legitimises itself as Christian and seeks to reproduce the identity of its citizens within this religious strategy, then those of other religions and to a lesser extent, those of no religion (Rudge, 1998), will be seen as outsiders, potentially as non-citizens. Conflicts between the mainly white, Christian nation and outsider groups such as Islam are not accidental but intrinsic to the state's religious and implicit nationalistic strategies in education.

Furthermore, similar polarisations between insiders and outsiders occur between those educated in the religified curriculum of the state and inhabitants of other states with other religions. The anti-Islamic climate prevalent across Europe needs to be acknowledged as at least in part produced by the religious strategy of states in educational institutions. In Europe, not least in schools and universities, the adjective Islamic and the nouns extremist or fundamentalist are far too readily linked. Non-pluralistic religious education has created an ignorance of the nature of Islam, its contribution to world, including European, history and civilisation and the current unhappy situation of many of its believers, in Bosnia and Tower Hamlets as well as in Palestine and Kashmir. This ignorance and prejudice is not unrelated to the practice of actual warfare as is shown by the contrast between the lethargy of the European Union military powers in intervening to save a Muslim population in Sarajevo and their speed and enthusiasm to intervene against an Islamic state in Iraq. The Gulf War example provides an opportunity to make explicit the extent of the argument in this part of the chapter. It was not the reinforcement of anti-Islamic prejudice in the schools and universities of Europe (and the USA) which brought about this war. The safety of the west's oil supply was a far more tangible reason. However, the existence of anti-Islamic prejudice made it easier for European populations to accept the necessity and rightness of the war. Religified curricula were by no means a sufficient cause of the war; they were, however, a necessary component of its initiation and continuation. Anti-Islamic prejudice is an important plank in European xenophobia. It is a central component in internal and external conflict. Far from seeking to reduce this prejudice, the school and university curricula in many European states, including those ostensibly secular, have functioned to encourage and perpetuate it.

Scientific research and development programmes

The science and technology taught in schools and especially universities is also explicitly linked to warfare. The key test here is, what do pupils and students do with science? To the extent - still minor - that young people actually use the science they have learned, it is within a limited range of occupations. School science prepares young people to be medical doctors or to be research scientists. Whilst, for this latter group, much of this research itself concerns medicine and pharmaceuticals, another large tranche of it consists in the development of military technology.

The classic example of scientific research in support of warfare is of course the Manhattan Project which developed the atomic bomb in World War Two (Gleick, 1994; Peieris, 1997; Rhodes, 1987). A more direct misapplication of science occurred during the Vietnam war when the United States military was faced with the difficulty that the victims of napalm attacks could actually brush the inflammable substance from their burning flesh. It was necessary to find a type of napalm that could not so easily be brushed off. Children progress from learning at primary school that oxygen is necessary for combustion to assessing ph values at secondary school and then to be young people who investigate the qualities of flammable substances at university. They may subsequently obtain successful employment, as a researcher, quite possibly in the same or another university, where they can develop ways in which napalm can be made more adhesive to the human skin. Indeed, much scientific research is actually conducted in universities, funded by governments, armament manufacturers and other providers of military technology. A well educated science 'community' working in fully equipped laboratories and with access to the latest learned journals is an indispensable component in the ability of states to wage modern, high-tech warfare, or to provide the materials whereby other states can thus dispose of their tax revenues. Scientific and technical education provides the tools of war.

The United States, the European Union, Japan and those other countries which consider themselves to be, or aspire to become, 'smart states' do so because they know that knowledge is increasingly the most valuable trading property in the global economy. Knowledge itself can be traded; it can also assist in the manufacture of other products that because of their technical superiority can command a high price or a large market or both. Pre-eminent among such products are armaments and military technology. From land mines, the low tech export of countries such as China, to the Hawk jets which British Aerospace provides to the Indonesian government for the domination of their civilian population, the arms trade is predicated on the provision of school and university science. Enlightenment science perceived itself to be a liberating agenda that would set humanity free from centuries of ignorance and superstition. In its most tangible and pre-eminent, current manifestations - Trident submarines, stealth bombers, cruise missiles - it has become via education and politics, one of the main tools of domination and aggression.

Science is also part of that ethnocentric and xenophobic knowledge which serves to facilitate the practice of warfare (Schneider, 1991). In this respect medicine and mathematics may also be brought into the argument which covers the trajectory of the objective knowledge developed by the Enlightenment. These were the areas in which Europeans were most certain that their knowledge was superior to and indeed truer than that of other, less enlightened people. The neglect of acknowledgement of non-European achievement and influence in science, mathematics and medicine is remarkable. Western science and mathematics are taught in European schools and universities as the one-true-way. There is little acknowledgement, for instance, that the Western number system is derived from the Arabs or the concept of zero from India (Joseph, 1992). There is little or no attention paid to non-western number systems. There is little attention given to other ranges of scientific explanation or methodology or to other conceptualisations of human health and the ways in which it may be maintained. This ethnocentric narrowness of focus has two important consequences: firstly, the nature of western science is limited and unnecessarily constrained in its access to the variety of international wisdom: secondly, because of the spectacular achievements of western science, not least in warfare, it forms the core component in the epistemological superiority complex so characteristic of Europeans and the west in general.

Nor are the actual activities and social functions of science, in terms of technical, exploitative interventions in the natural world or of the development of the global armoury, investigated. In medicine, discussed from another perspective in Chapter Five, the pharmaceutical and surgical paradigms are paramount. Despite the popularity and proliferation of alternative therapies in the United States and the European Union, these receive little acknowledgement in the university medicine curriculum. Invasive surgery and post-Freudian psychoanalysis are medical science; acupuncture and homeopathy are mere 'complementary' therapies. More importantly, European medicine teaches, to patients and clinicians alike, a notion of human health predicated upon illness and professional intervention. It sees health only in terms of its opposite and treatment as individual and atomistic. It has little conception of health as a component of all life, no matter the degree of clinical or aesthetic impairment, as something generated in interaction with family, community and the awareness of living creatures and landscapes. In this way science and medicine have placed constraints on the way in which Europeans live, their access to a wider conception of health and their understanding of what it is to be human.

Whilst mathematics, science and medicine may not be curriculum areas which evidence petty state nationalisms, they are part of a wider western xenophobia which finds it difficult to acknowledge achievement outside its own paradigm and which, in particular, is loath to recognise the cultural, scientific and political achievements of Africa and Asia. In facilitating the belief that real, true, hard knowledge originates only in the west, the teaching of science, mathematics and medicine facilitate the economic and, if necessary military, domination of other parts of the world.

Military training

Military training, discussed in more detail in Chapter Seven, is itself actually a component of much of education throughout the world. Perhaps the most extreme current example is Venezuela where President Chavez (himself a former paratrooper and leader of a military coup) has recently decreed that all children must be given military training. In both primary and secondary schools children are to be instructed in military strategy, weapons handling and issues of national sovereignty (Gamini, 1999). But military training does not need to be quite so explicit as this. A good deal of standing up and saluting the flag or shouting and marching about in yards is done in schools and universities in Europe without any explicit reference to military activity. Collective acts of assembly or worship often involve national or military insignia or reference. Playground games follow the dramas and personalities of the state's latest military adventure. Often toys and equipment provided by playgroups, schools or other benevolent authorities encourage and facilitate the emulation of military behaviour from a very young age (Dixon, 1990). In this respect play and toys form one of the earlier gendering experiences of European children. It is boys in particular who are given guns, model military aircraft, action men and military uniforms as appropriate play equipment. The development of commercial ICT has spawned military flight simulators, military games and conquest scenario games in various formats from hand held machines through to the latest Pentium technology. Again it is overwhelmingly boys who are encouraged to take an interest in such products.

Physical education and sports accustom children and young people to the disciplining of the body so central to military service. In England and Wales physical education used to be referred to, revealingly, as drill. They help to establish the values of teamwork, co-operative competition and esprit de corps. The very format of invasive team games mimics the 18th century battlefield. They cultivate a fitness and athleticism that is one of the necessary components of militarism. This athleticism also has its ideological dimension: toughness and ruthlessness as well as muscularity are internalised as masculine virtues. The internalisation of military virtues is essential for those who will not ultimately be service people as well as for those who will. Obviously compulsory military national service for all in many European countries assists with this ideological process of the legitimation of warfare. (The current decline in conscription across Europe is not so much a sign of increasing peacefulness as a reflection of the need for a greater level of professionalism in Europe's armed forces.) Physical education and team sports further encourage a competitiveness within and between institutions which so readily leads to the frenzied chauvinism of national level tournaments in sports such as rugby or football or even the Olympic Games. As the Duke of Wellington remarked, the Battle of Waterloo was won on the playing fields of Eton.

Training in conformity

The ways in which schools reproduce patterns of authority and conformity are familiar themes of the sociology of education (Grace, 1978). In some cases this has been linked to the perceived requirements of a workforce within the capitalist system (Bowles and Gintis, 1976). It is more obviously, as well as more generally, linked to the requirements of a militarised population. Although now abandoned in many European states for the reason mentioned earlier, conscription remains a feature of the lives of many young people in Europe, including those states as ostensibly peaceful and stable as the Netherlands and Switzerland. In transitional states such as Russia, conscription, though profoundly unpopular, is, with education, one of the foundations of nation building. In order for a population to accept the astonishing infringement of personal liberty represented by the disciplines of conscription, and for young people to consent to it with little or no hesitation, earlier forms of social control are clearly essential. To the extent that schools and universities help to produce an obedient, conformist population, they assist in ensuring people's consent for, and indeed participation in, the act of warfare.

Mass warfare and mass education are both aspects of modernity. The *levee en masse* and the products of the industrial revolution transformed warfare from an activity of small professional armed forces into total war that engages entire economies and populations. Educational institutions became in the 19th century the chosen means by which the philosophy of the Enlightenment was transmitted and developed. Whilst the link between the two processes were rarely explicit, they were able to coexist in harmony if not symbiosis. The schooled, young English volunteers who walked so readily over the top on the first day of the Somme offensive, the scientifically educated Germans who developed the gas and the bureaucratic/industrial system necessary for the death camps, the technical self-sufficiency which ensured the rapid re-industrialisation of the eastern Soviet Union and provided the materials for the Red Army's break out from the Volga, all hang together as part of a society in which education, material production and warfare are the three central components, whatever the political ideology.

Although the nature of warfare appears to have changed within Europe, in that mass inter-state wars thankfully appear to be a thing of the past, events in places like former Yugoslavia suggest that progress away from mass conflict within European is not the given it was thought to be some twenty years ago. They also suggest that European schooling systems maintain practices that can support such outbreaks of mass violence.

Among the issues considered in the final chapter is the postmodernist critique of enlightenment knowledge. As this critique of knowledge gathers force in the educational discourse, it may be that different forms of education, if not of warfare, may emerge. Whilst a postmodernist curriculum is far from identifiable in any European state, the knowledge system on which it might be based is now visible. Postmodernist knowledge systems acknowledge not only the international contribution to Western civilisation but also that Western knowledge systems themselves must be placed within an international context of which the West is but a part. Postmodern knowledge systems recognise the importance of women in the formation of history, culture and knowledge. They recognise the wealth of different knowledges, sciences and cultures that are in dialogue and conflict. Such systems are intrinsically international in a way in which western traditional and modernist systems have failed to be. School and university knowledge have been vital elements in the reproduction of ethnocentrism and warfare. It is possible that they could be just as powerful elements in their reversal and ultimate elimination. The postmodernist critique and its version of a pluralistic, contested, manifold, provisional knowledge may offer the most positive alternative for curricular systems. It may serve to begin to erode ethnocentrism and provide a more humane version of science, and thereby to diminish the likelihood of warfare.

Warfare is ongoing in Europe: civil strife in Corsica, the Basque country and Northern Ireland; genocide and ethnic cleansing and associated NATO responses in Bosnia and Kosovo; post-imperial adventures such as Iraq or the Malvinas/Falkland Islands. Wider conflict waits ever dangerously in the wings as evidenced by the Russian response to the NATO intervention on Kosovo or Greek and Turkish sabre-rattling over obscure Aegean islands. In Europe, the joke has it, countries go to war not to control the future but to control the past. There is a depressing accuracy to this. The main place where the past – thus controlled by the victors - is reproduced, is the school and university curriculum. It is then both the beginning and ending of warfare. Modern European states, thankfully, will rarely go to war unless their tangible political and economic interests are threatened. Even then the nationalism and xenophobia supplied by the school and university curriculum may be a necessary, though not sufficient, element in the mobilisation of the population, and especially those called on to fight, in the acceptance of warfare. In states thrown by transition into outbreaks of traditionalist fervour, notably Serbia, the school and university curriculum along with religious institutions and the state-controlled media may become the main strands in the formation and reproduction of a xenophobic nationalism capable of undertaking any military extremity or barbarity. Where schools and universities have taught nationalism and hatred they are not innocent of their involvement in European warfare.

Wilfred Owen wrote this reproof to Horace and this advice to educators from the Western Front in 1917. The narrator cannot escape dreams of a comrade who has been the victim of a mustard gas attack and pleads:

> In all my dreams, before my helpless sight,
> He plunges at me, guttering, choking, drowning.
>
> If in some smothering dreams you too could pace
> Behind the wagon that we flung him in,
> And watch the white eyes writhing in his face,
> His hanging face, like a devil's sick of sin;
> If you could hear, at every jolt, the blood
> Come gargling from the froth-corrupted lungs,
> Obscene as cancer, bitter as the cud
> Of vile, incurable sores on innocent tongues, -
> My friend, you would not tell with such high zest
> To children ardent for some desperate glory,
> The old Lie: Dulce et decorum est
> Pro patria mori.

In parts of Europe, some 80 years after Owen wrote this, the 'old Lie' is still being told.

5 Knowledge, Prejudice and Special Educational Needs

What becomes clear in looking at education systems like that of Bosnia-Herzegovina, that collapse as a result of warfare or violence (an example discussed in more detail in Chapter 10), is that children with special educational needs suffer first and longest. Their traditional marginalisation is compounded by war. But there is a reason for this, it is not just chance. This chapter therefore examines the curricula and assessment systems of schools and universities in Europe with regard to their function in legitimating and embodying particular views of special educational need. (The concept of need in this categorisation is not taken for granted but opened to question below.) Other authors have examined the ways in which the processes and indeed the structures of schooling serve to pick out some children and young adults as being, in whatever way, different (Garner and Sandow, 1995a, 1995b). These differences then become the focus for educational interventions in the learning, the life style and indeed the life chances of the individuals concerned. What differentiates this individual from others, rather than what s/he may have in common with them, then becomes the focus for intense educational, or medical, psychological, psychiatric etc, interest and activity.

Much remains to be done to rectify these processes and structures. It is the contention of this chapter, however, that these processes and structures themselves are underpinned by knowledge systems and knowledge protocols which, in so far as they impact on children and young people perceived to have special educational needs, have remained largely unchallenged. Central to them is the differentiation of school populations, a generally well-meaning process that often encourages a negative view of the different. (The history and practice of Eugenics is instructive in this respect.) This chapter examines firstly knowledge systems and then knowledge protocols that encourage, albeit unwittingly in most cases, this negative and potentially dangerous state of affairs.

Knowledge systems: science and normality

As mentioned in Chapter Four and explored further in Chapter Six, knowledge systems have been subjected to a critique from a position which might be broadly categorised as postmodernist. Modernist knowledge has been seen as being sexist: it is knowledge about men, men's activities, achievements and interests, constructed by men, according to criteria and values which are important to men. Much of this knowledge has links to warfare as well, a particularly male interest. The roles of women in knowledge and the criteria they might apply to its construction and organisation have largely been ignored. Similarly, as far back as Marx, knowledge and culture had been seen to be those skills, products and activities most pleasing to the ruling class of any particular epoch and most likely to assist in the extension of their wealth and power. In Chapter Four traditionalist and modernist knowledge systems in Europe were characterised as Eurocentric, white, racist and having the sometimes-explicit propensity to support violence and warfare.

Parallel critiques have been made from a variety of particular positions: to take two more examples, gay rights and environmentalism. Knowledge has been seen to privilege heterosexual forms of human relationships. The achievement of homosexual people in cultural, scientific, political and other areas has been concealed, disguised, marginalised or sanitised. The extreme is the fact that homosexuals were one of the chief groups the Nazis tried to exterminate. Homophobic prejudice has been reinforced by school and university knowledge. The way in which the aids scare has been transposed into health education is an example of this. Health education plays into the media presentation of HIV as a disease of *others* - Africans, drug users, and homosexuals. Existing fears and even hatreds are thus given medical justification.

Environmentalists and eco-feminists have also found modernist versions of knowledge inadequate to meet the crises of unequal distribution and pollutive and unsustainable production. The knowledge of schools and universities, they assert, is almost exclusively that which will perpetuate modes of production and consumption which exacerbate the ecological crises. Modernist knowledge as transmitted in European schools and universities does not offer forms of production and behaviour that might serve to avert or at least diminish these crises (Hicks and Slaughter, 1998).

A further critique of modernist knowledge with regard to people who are perceived in various ways to be disabled is still emerging (Daniels and Garner, 1999). It is of particular importance to the institutions of education since these are the sites where knowledge is legitimated and reproduced for those perceived to be disabled.

Equally, but not so obviously important, they are the sites where knowledge is legitimated and reproduced for those not so perceived, indeed for those making the perception. In this respect, this chapter focuses on science and in particular medicine. However, it is a mode of analysis that needs to be conducted with regard to a whole range of curricular areas. How much of the literature studied in schools and universities, for instance, has been written by people perceived to be disabled? To what extent does the educational canon of literature accurately reflect the experiences of such people, distort these experiences or ignore them altogether (*Jane Eyre, Jude the Obscure, The Idiot*)? Parallel, though less easily formulated questions can be asked of music and art *(Lucia di L'ammermoor, Boris Godunov, The Scream)*. The romanticisation and marginalisation of madness is not without influence on the process of identity formation.

In a similar way, to what extent does school and university history address the circumstances of people perceived to be disabled and their relationships with each other and with people not so perceived? What provisions and institutions were created for them? What philosophies underpinned and legitimated these forms and processes? In this case, of course, Foucault has provided some of the answers. However, the Foucauldian view of *Madness and Civilisation* and *The Birth of the Clinic* is not one that has progressed very far in the European school and university history curriculum (Foucault, 1967; 1973).

In all subjects the questions of representation and especially inclusion remain. To what extent do examples and illustrations in science and technology texts emphasise the activities, achievements and potentialities of those perceived to be disabled? Stephen Hawking has recently become, at least in the UK, a widely known example of such achievement. To what extent does the discourse of educational subject knowledge across the school and university curriculum stress the arrangements, facilities and technologies necessary to facilitate total inclusion? It is the argument of this chapter that it is school and university knowledge as a whole, but particularly the university study of medicine and educational psychology, which produce and legitimate special educational need as well as the wider patterns of stratification examined in preceding chapters.

It is science, especially the university level subjects of medicine and educational psychology, which is the central subject with regard to the way in which school and university knowledge excludes and stigmatises those perceived to be disabled. Medical students at London University are privileged to be able to visit a collection of 'freaks' (scare quotes proliferate in this area). The skeleton of 'the Elephant Man', for instance, has not been respectfully laid to rest but is there for the critical attention of such students. Their scrutiny did not end with death. What is here in an extreme form is a set of confusions that underpin western medicine. Health is associated inextricably with normality. Health and normality are associated with well-being and even with benevolence. It is the opposite formulation of these confusions which effect people perceived to be 'disabled': difference from the artificially constructed normal is equated with sickness, with misfortune and, again more tendentiously, with malevolence. In the reverse process, that which is criminal or wicked is seen as being necessarily unhealthy or unbalanced (Szasz, 1972) - consider the use of words such as 'twisted', 'psycho' or 'sick'.

It is science here which makes the association which literature and popular culture can readily take up and amplify in the strand which ties the unusual to the malevolent via sickness (the psychopath, for instance, in crime fiction or Hollywood movies, the association of 'deformity' with evil from *Richard III* to *Don't Look Now*). This Platonic link between disability and evil is of long standing in European culture. Shakespeare's contemporary, Francis Bacon, is typical of this perspective in his essay *Of Deformity*:

> *Deformed persons* are commonly even with Nature: For as Nature hath done ill by them; So doe they by Nature; Being for the most part, (as the Scripture saith) void of *Natural Affection*; And so they have their revenge of Nature (Bacon, 1937, p. 179).

Despite rejecting such a view, much modern educational and medical practice still supports similar stigmatisation. The medicine which is taught at universities in Europe and the school science which feeds into it is a knowledge system which supports the segregation and stigmatisation of those perceived to be different both in educational institutions and, far from unconnectedly, in wider society. As Illich asserted:

> With the development of the therapeutic service sector of the economy, an increasing proportion of all people come to be perceived as deviating from some desirable norm, and therefore as clients who can now either be submitted to therapy to bring them closer to the established standard

of health or concentrated into some special environment
built to cater to their deviance (Illich, 1976, p. 72).

School and university science does this because it is committed to
a notion of normality that is restricted in terms of physical, behavioural and
even cosmetic conformity. Its attitude and response to that which fails to
conform to its normality may be prurient, excluding, invasive, stigmatising
and often punitive. More to the point of this book, not being perceived as
'normal' justifies a range of negative attitudes and actions, including,
ultimately, violent responses, as the right wing attacks in Germany on both
'foreigners' and people with disabilities in wheel chairs demonstrates. To
substantiate this rather large statement the argument in this chapter goes on
to consider four of the main tools of western medicine: pharmaceuticals,
invasive surgery, 'counselling' and pre-natal screening.

Pharmaceuticals, for all the good that most of them do, are also
increasingly being used to control people's behaviour and even emotions.
Pills and medication help people to sleep, to behave in a socially acceptable
way, to feel good about themselves and to be happy. Pharmaceuticals such
as Prozac and Ritalin, are used as a first level intervention to control
behaviour in increasingly large numbers of children and young people.
Tranquillisers and anti-depressants are considered necessary treatment for
people who have suffered serious physical injury or who are considered to
be physically disabled. Tolerance of a wide range of behaviours is
constantly diminishing.

The history of enforced lobotomies, sterilisations (as late as the
1960s in Sweden) and castrations recalls that medical surgery has also been
used to control behaviour. Plastic surgery provides an example of the
relationship between medicine and normality enforcement, in this case
cosmetic. Surgery is used to eliminate perceived disfigurement, ugliness
and abnormality. In the process it is clear that youth, normality and beauty
are medically endorsed as components of human health. Medicine, aided
and abetted by psychoanalysis, has proliferated a sequence of categories for
people whose behaviour differs from and upsets the norm: psychotic,
schizophrenic, depressive, autistic, dyslexic, etc. These categories are used
to describe, stigmatise and treat behavioural, sexual, legal and even
political (in the former Soviet Union, say) deviations from the norms of
'mental health'. Surgical and pharmaceutical interventions have been
justified for such deviations. Even more radical solutions towards those
perceived to have special needs have been adopted by several European
states during the last century: Mazower cites a Nazi text in a quotation
which, by implicating the social priorities of the Third Reich, brings many

themes of this book together: '"The construction of a lunatic asylum costs 6 million RM. How many houses at 15,000 RM each could have been built for that amount?" a maths school book asked children' (Mazower, 1998, p. 99).

The people concerned in these particular pharmaceutical and surgical interventions - clients or victims - may also be subjected to waves of medical or para-medical 'counselling'. If your body or behaviour do not match medical and social 'normality', or even if you are in the process of enduring grief or unhappiness, then you are a candidate for counselling. Counselling reminds you subtly what the norm is, sympathises with you for your failure to achieve it, instructs you how to handle your various inadequacies so as not to offend the normal and how to conform in the future in as many ways as counselling considers you capable.

Prenatal screening, amniocentesis and ultrasound, allow an increasing number of deviations from the medical norm to be recognised and diagnosed before birth. Where Downs Syndrome is diagnosed abortion may be almost routine in such cases. The social consequences of such abortions are that there are now categories of people whose whole existence may be regarded as a medical mistake. If a child is fortunate enough to survive a condition where medicine would routinely terminate a pregnancy, how is s/he and others to regard the condition of their existence? Is human life only to be allowed to those whom medicine regards to be normal? Medicine has shifted the Nazi notion of 'purification' into the prenatal phase where it apparently remains socially acceptable. As it is now possible to determine other characteristics, not least gender, at an early stage in pregnancy, the possibility emerges of the made-to-order baby, with all models that do not fit the specification, peremptorily terminated. Genetic engineering, further, holds the possibility of the exclusive propagation of the scientific normal.

It may be argued that this is being selective in the aspects of medicine which are portrayed; that this is bad medicine but that most of European, modernist medicine is good: antibiotics, for instance, and miracle surgery. These two examples, of course, are not without their negative aspects: the degradation of antibiotics by their systematic use on farm animals in Europe and the United States; the routine and superfluous implementation of procedures such as tonsillectomies. The stress of the argument here, however, is rather that, if the aspects of medicine described and questioned in the above paragraphs are recognisable components, and actually rather significant components, then the whole edifice of European, modernist medicine is flawed. This applies not only in relation to those perceived to be disabled but also in relation to those not (yet) so perceived.

It is not being asserted that there is no such thing as health and sickness nor even as real disablement: rather it is insisted that, in western medicine, these concepts have maintained their links with socially derived notions of normality, conformity, beauty, happiness and even moral worth. This renders their continued implementation as theory and practice prejudicial to the population at large and in particular to that segment of it perceived to be disabled.

It is in educational institutions, principally in universities and university hospitals across Europe, that this version of medicine is taught. It is important to emphasise, however, that this does not involve only university medical schools. Aspects of medicine are now taught to a whole range of would be para-medical professionals. Furthermore, medicine is seen to be one of the peaks of modernist science; it constitutes, in the European Union, one of the most desirable and most difficult to attain careers for those pupils and students most successful within education systems. In universities it is usually recognised as an elite subject; medical courses are characteristically longer than most others; those who teach on them are frequently paid at a higher level than other academics. One of the important functions of school science is the preparation of young people for these medical and paramedical courses. Schools and universities not only teach modernist medicine, they also teach that this form of conceptualisation, diagnosis and treatment is right, good and desirable. Other modes of diagnosis, aetiology and therapy (acupuncture, homeopathy, faith healing, herbalism etc.) are ignored, marginalised or denigrated. The actual construction of the school and university curriculum, then, underpins those conceptualisations, processes and institutions which have been so prejudicial to people perceived to be disabled.

A trend in much writing on special educational needs has been to criticise, rightly, the application of what has been called the medical model in cases where it is deemed to be inappropriate (Sandow, 1994). With regard to upsetting behaviour or to underachievement in school, for instance, it has been recognised that the use of medical terminology and procedures, far from assisting either understanding or intervention, is quite likely to be harmful to the people to whom they are applied. It does this both by offering possibilities for stigmatisation and also by taking the responsibility away from those most closely involved in working with the child or young person, almost always parents or carers and teachers. This chapter is arguing something somewhat beyond this: that it is not the inappropriate application of the medical model which is the difficulty, but the whole medical model itself and the European, modernist version of medicine and science which underpins it. Both as a version of scientific knowledge and as an institutionalised professional practice, this modernist medicine has been highly prejudicial to, among others, those children and young people perceived to have special educational needs.

In wider terms, of course, it can be seen as being prejudicial to everyone. As well as more general matters such as the morbid concern with health, beauty and fitness, so prevalent in Europe, there are more specific issues which concern children and young people perceived to have special educational needs. The tendency to medicalise and stigmatise any form of deviation from the norm restricts everyone's version of what it is to be a human being. This restriction is compounded by the institutional arrangements of segregated schooling. Since so many children and young people in mainstream schools are not educated alongside their disabled peers, they do not learn about them, about their experiences or about ways in which they can collaborate with them. Their notion of what it is to be a human being falls within the highly restricted 'normality' of the medical model. The curriculum of the non-disabled is thus severely restricted, a restriction which, in its turn serves to enhance the credibility of the medical model.

Knowledge protocols: stratification and normality

The term knowledge protocols refers to the way in which school knowledge is selected, organised, valued and assessed. Again there is a range of issues derived from the postmodernist critique of modernist knowledge which can be seen to be relevant to the education of children and young people perceived to have special educational needs. Underachievement is most frequently seen to be an attribute of the pupil or student concerned. It is a result of their (tautologically) perceived 'ability'. The victim is firmly blamed. But might it not be determined by the nature of the knowledge that is selected to be taught in schools and universities or by the way in which it is organised? If a different aspect of knowledge were selected - co-operative and environment-enhancing, say, as against competitive and exploitative - or if it were organised differently - in an integrated, holistic way, for example, rather than in distinctly separated subjects - might not those currently perceived as underachieving be seen as successful and an entirely different group of pupils be discovered to be underachievers? If this revolution were to be achieved might there not be predictable but different winners and losers in terms of 'race', gender or social class? Certainly there are cross-cultural differences in the status awarded to particular cognitive activities (Labov, 1969). As discussed in earlier chapters, different groups have different notions of what constitutes knowledge. In considering the underpinnings of the prejudicial conceptualisations, processes and institutions of special educational needs, these issues remain to be addressed. Thus, the rest of this chapter is concerned with two knowledge protocols, those of assessment and intelligence, because these are the ones which are of particular negative relevance to children and young people perceived to have special needs.

Assessment - tests, examinations, checks on individuals' learning and learning patterns - is an important protocol for modernist knowledge. It allows educational institutions to recognise those who are succeeding and those who are failing. It allows for success to be rewarded and failure to be addressed. It allows rational, generalist decisions to be made instead of traditional particularist favouritism. Such decisions are easier to defend in democratic, open societies. The opening of the civil service in the United Kingdom to entrance by competitive examinations, in the mid-19th century, rather than by social sponsorship, is an example of the liberal, progressive policy-making favoured by the Enlightenment. Assessment, as a modernist protocol, opens, in the Napoleonic formulation, careers to talent; provides an apparently rational filtering mechanism for successive levels of educational and professional promotion and allows for 'remedial' action for those seen visibly and measurably to be failing.

Also in England and Wales the implementation of the National Curriculum and its associated testing arrangements, has recently industrialised the assessment process. All school age children are assessed in at least three subjects at at least four points during their school careers on tests, which are set, marked and, at least to the satisfaction of government politicians, standardised nationally. The result of this industry is that all school age children can be calibrated, to the delight of journalists as well as politicians, according to their progress in at least three subjects. Data are available to compare them to the norm of their own school, of their LEA and of England and Wales as a whole, again in at least three subjects. The results of these assessments are regularly communicated to teachers and to parents or carers but, for the latter group, only in terms of their individual children. The results of other children in the class and school are meant to be confidential. Conversations between parents or carers and children as well as playground gossip by both parties, mean that the results, even for individuals, rapidly have some public currency. In terms of aggregate results for schools and for LEAs, these data are now routinely tabulated by government and media into league tables. The publication of league tables of the National Curriculum test results and of GCSE and 'A'-level grades are a regular media event.

These centralised assessment and publication arrangements set in motion at least two further educational processes, competition and stratification. These are not unforeseen outcomes of the 1988 legislation which introduced the National Curriculum, rather they are part of its clear intentions (Chitty, 1989). The assessment sets child against child, teacher against teacher, school against school and LEA against LEA in a competition to get the highest scores. Those who formulated and adopted the Act believed in the positive social consequences of competition in its own right: it was a central component of their knowledge protocol (Bash and Coulby, 1989; Coulby and Bash, 1991). They considered that, in educational terms, these competitions would serve to raise standards of attainment.

With regard to stratification, the assessment arrangements highlight the successes and failures of each individual and, although this is rarely officially investigated, of ethnic minorities (Gillborn and Youdell, 2000). Again this was seen as positive since the perpetrators of the Act were committed to an ideology of individual difference whereby some people are more 'intelligent' than others and thus are more successful in schools and universities and thence in the wider society and economy. (A fundamental flaw in the current debate, or more accurately lack of debate, about the (un)desirability of mixed ability teaching in secondary schools is that it utilises the highly questionable concept of ability, 'intelligence', as if it were a taken for granted truth.) This hierarchy, apparently reasonably enough, being reflected in subsequent life chances. The assessment arrangements make visible the hierarchy of success of pupils from a very early age and that, for New Labour as well as for the Tory enactors of the National Curriculum, is how life apparently is.

This theory of individual difference, with its reliance on a notion of generalisable intelligence or ability ('gifted pupils', 'the less able', 'remedial' and so on), is itself a product of modernity. The science of intelligence and its associated modes of calibration, not to mention fundamentally racist and sexist assumptions, was developed by psychologists working around the turn of the century (Simon, 1971). It is an important component of the underpinnings of educational psychology in the United Kingdom, and elsewhere in Europe, today. More generally it informs the day-to-day assumptions, lexical frameworks and modes of judgement not only of politicians but also of many teachers and lecturers. The notion of intelligence is a centrally important knowledge protocol within modernist education. The literature which exposes intelligence as a political rather than a scientific construct is familiar (classically, Kamin, 1974). There is no such thing as intelligence. Human beings perform various intellectual and non-intellectual tasks with varying degrees of skill, according to their background, interests and enthusiasm. Very few people are successful in many areas. Very few fail in many. Educational institutions, as well as families, themselves play an important part in determining what level of interest and enthusiasm will be brought to bear upon a particular task. Equally important to this chapter is the insistence that what is seen to be 'intelligence', that is performance on a range of high status, high visibility tests, is itself dependent upon decisions made within other knowledge protocols. If knowledge had been differently selected, valued or organised then other and different pupils would have been the more successful in performance, that is, would have been more 'intelligent'.

The knowledge protocol of differential intelligence is itself taught and studied in European universities especially within the discipline of educational psychology. Educational psychology, as a discursive strategy, attempts to schematise human difference in behaviour and performance, especially with regard to children and young people, and relate these to biological differences rather than to social and economic circumstances. This atomistic approach is currently being reinforced by the rapid developments in genetics. Newspaper headlines that inform the public that homosexuality - to take but one absurd example - is genetically transmitted ensure that this knowledge protocol is more popularly available. It is people trained within educational psychology who are often the professionals used by educational systems in testing for various perceived disabilities in terms of performance and behaviour. How they explain the disproportionate number of Roma children in special schools across South-eastern Europe is an interesting question.

The discipline of educational psychology has an even wider significance. In many countries in Europe it forms an important component of the education of teachers. Teachers' notions about behavioural conformity and about the differential 'intelligence' of their pupils are thus part of their professional preparation and legitimated by this area of university knowledge. Given the role of teachers in the processes of stigmatisation and stratification described in this chapter, educational psychology is perhaps an essential professional legitimation. Certainly the reversal of these processes in the progress towards a more inclusive and comprehensive school system requires an entirely different philosophical framework from that derived from educational psychology (for a wide range of non-UK examples, see the essays in Daniels and Garner, 1999).

One of the consequences of the assessment protocol is the stratification of children and young people. Central to this part of the chapter are the effects of stratification on pupils' lives. These effects can be summarised under three categories:

- the facilitation of labelling;
- the legitimation of the existence of many of the categories of special educational needs;
- the inhibition of inclusive education policies.

These three themes are examined in turn.

Assessment arrangements often provide a ready label for each child. For example, in England and Wales, a 'level oner' is the new label given to children achieving the lowest attainment level in the English and Welsh national tests. Less specific labels, 'not-very-good-at-maths', 'low ability' often carry the endorsement of government sponsored judgement since they result from the apparently scientific and rational testing or the professional judgement of teachers. In both cases there is industrial back up, the testing industry or the teacher training and accreditation industry. It would be difficult for parents or carers to resist the accuracy of such powerfully legitimated professional labels and to insist that the child in question is actually rather good at maths. Even less could they argue that the whole notion of ability is politically and educationally fraudulent and retrograde and should therefore never be applied to their child or, for that matter, to any other. More likely the parents or carers and then the children themselves accept the label from an early age and start living with ways of adapting to both it and its consequences. A critically important way in which they will adapt to the label is by not risking the failure that would be involved in attempting to challenge it. The child will accept the not-very-good-at-maths label, may even come to relish it, and thenceforth will feel extenuated from making too much effort in school mathematics. The result of this relaxation of effort, of course, will apparently be to make the judgement retrospectively correct. An apparent correctness likely to be repeated and further entrenched by each successive round of assessment.

The processes of self-fulfilling labelling have been described before as have the ways in which pupils internalise the labels used about them (Hargreaves and et al, 1975). The apparent fulfilment of the label appears to legitimate its use, proves that it is 'true'. By internalising the label, the subject of it gives the whole process a further level of authenticity. When a pupil accepts the label that s/he is not-very-good-at-maths this has consequences for subsequent educational and almost certainly economic success. But failure at school and in the workplace can be made to seem fair and correct: it is justifiable because 'I was not-very-good-at-maths'. This then places the burden of responsibility on the individual child and removes any blame or indeed possibility of positive action from educational institutions, their processes and personnel. In internalising the label the subject defends her/himself against the hurt of educational, social and economic failure and their associated stigma. The assessment system is seen to be just and the subject can acknowledge her/his place in a hierarchy with the minimum amount of stress. 'I failed at school because I was not-very-good-at-maths but I am happy about what I did. It is nobody's fault but my own. But that's the sort of person I am' (that is basically okay). Instead of labelling then being identified as one of the causes of educational underachievement, it is taken on, by both agents and victims alike, as 'proof' that the system is just and that everybody is happy. It is for children perceived to have special educational needs that these processes have particular power.

Those consistently at the lowest end of the performance scale in the school or national tests will have labels applied to them even more pernicious and enduring than not-very-good-at-maths. In segregative school systems, such as that of England (see OFSTED, 1999 for the latest situation), such labels can all too often be transformed into institutional arrangements ('remedial' classes, schools for children with moderate or severe 'learning difficulties' etc.) whereby pupils are subjected to a restricted curriculum and a negatively selected peer group.

As well as the consequences for individual pupils, national curriculum and assessment arrangements and associated testing regimes, often masquerading as diagnostic screening, function to legitimate whole categories of perceived special educational need through 'low attainers' groups via 'remedial' classes to 'moderate and severe learning difficulty'. The differential performance on national tests, increasingly a feature of European education systems, prove, to both agent and victim alike, what those inculcated in the discipline of educational psychology already know, that people have different natural abilities. The tests, by definition, ensure that there is always a category of children who are at the lowest level of this stratification. They demonstrate that this category of pupils 'needs' (for of course this whole notion of special educational need should itself have been in scare quotes from the very start) a different form of educational provision, preferably segregated from the rest of the age cohort and ideally in a separate institution out of sight and out of mind.

And in legitimating one form of special need all the others too are brought into more concrete conceptual and institutional existence. Once there is a 'science' which taxonomises children according to their perceived ability/need/disability, then other forms of difference, blindness or a tendency to upsetting behaviour, say, can be all brought in as other sub-categories of this rational and ameliorative science.

The category of special educational needs is entirely one of ascription. The need is in no sense derived from the individual social or economic need of the child or young person under scrutiny (for a square meal, for instance, or to be removed from a physically and sexually abusing environment). The need is derived from the disciplines of medicine and educational psychology which position individuals along scales of normality with regard to behaviour, performance and appearance and which are highly intolerant of those who fall at the bottom end of their self-perpetuating taxonomies. More crudely the need can be derived from the institutional arrangements which these professionals will deem appropriate. A headteacher desires that a troublesome, underperforming child be removed from mainstream school; an obliging psychologist discovers that the child has a low 'IQ'; the child is sent to a segregated school for slow learners (various euphemistic designations). As part of this process the child is discovered to need specialist teaching away from the excitements of mainstream school. The provision that the system intends to impose is legitimated as what the child needs. The fact that the children and young people subjected to these processes are almost exclusively working class (Ford et al., 1982) and disproportionately black (Tomlinson, 1981; Tomlinson, 1982) is hidden in the ameliorative, pseudo-scientific processes which conceal themselves in the discourse of meeting individual needs. Special educational needs in too many countries of Europe have been used as a way to stigmatise and exclude particular groups (Westwood, 1994).

Romania provides a further example of the racial aspect of segregated special provision as well as the ways in which provision made often with the best of intentions may, in the event, serve to further disadvantage some children and groups. Romania has made a separate provision for Roma children to allow them to have intensive help in their education and then return to mainstream children. Although this provision is theoretically for all impoverished children it is actually almost exclusively Roma who attend. Although they are meant to be reintegrated into mainstream school this rarely happens. Furthermore, the nature of the provision, the curriculum followed and the training of the teachers is identical with that associated with the special education of children with severe learning difficulties (McDonald, 1999). Three things then happen: firstly, segregationist education of Roma children is legitimated on the basis of their special need; secondly, all Roma children and indeed Roma people can all too easily be identified with children with severe learning difficulties. Thirdly, and perhaps most importantly, the segregation of

Roma children enables prejudice to flourish unchallenged to the point that violence against Roma people becomes socially understandable if not wholly acceptable (Bridge, 1993).

Lest this last paragraph be seen as the comforting western stereotype about the unfortunate Romanian gypsies, a recent press report indicates a parallel situation in the Czech Republic where Roma children are fifteen times more likely than Czech children to be placed in schools for 'the mentally retarded'. Roma rights campaigners are taking the Czech Ministry of Education to court over the issue in a move which parallels American black activists' struggle to break down the segregative provision for black children thirty years ago (Glass, 1999). Indeed, across Europe, Roma people's general social exclusion is usually confirmed and supported by the education that is given to their children.

England and Wales has a rigidly segregationist tradition for the education of children perceived to have special needs (Bash, Coulby, and Jones, 1985) and the wider consequences of the assessment arrangements introduced by the 1988 Act have been used further to inhibit the development of inclusive schools. The published test results are not the record of an abstract competition: there is a real and tangible prize. It is assumed, with only some degree of accuracy, that parents and carers will use the published test results, the league tables, when selecting schools for their children. Since funding now automatically accompanies pupil numbers, by a parallel provision of the 1988 Act, schools are, in the main, anxious to recruit as many children and young people as they possibly can. This is not only a test of popularity, it is the way of ensuring continuing employment for teachers and buoyant budgets for academic activities. Primary and secondary schools are therefore looking increasingly cautiously at pupils who are likely significantly to reduce their aggregate test scores. It is of course the more 'successful' (in terms of the tests) schools that can afford to be thus discriminating/discriminatory. The other schools must take what pupils they can find. Those children and young people who are scoring at the very bottom end of the tests, however, are increasingly unattractive to all schools. This applies even more to those pupils whom schools consider to be likely to impede the scores of other children due to the extent of their upsetting behaviour. The assessment arrangements actually constitute a disincentive, within the education system as a whole, to the creation of inclusive schools. Instead they function to perpetuate the demand, from teachers, headteachers and even parents or carers in mainstream schools, for exclusion and for segregative provision.

It is European knowledge systems and their associated protocols, at least as much as the embedded institutional arrangements which they underpin, that are responsible for legitimating and reproducing prejudicial attitudes towards children and young people perceived to have special educational needs. Prejudice and stereotyping are processes intrinsic to the modernist knowledge system. This has been recognised and challenged by increasing numbers of groups that the knowledge systems attempted to reduce to victims, inferiors, patients, perverts etc. The challenge on behalf of children and young people perceived to have special educational needs is taking place within and beyond schools and universities. As well as developing a critique of modernist knowledge, this challenge needs to develops and publicise accounts of non-prejudicial ways of constituting, organising, legitimating, sharing and evaluating knowledge and knowledge systems (Coulby and Coulby, 1995). That is to say, it will need to develop new, non-prejudicial knowledge protocols that can lead to a more inclusive understanding of what it is to be a human being. It is this lack of inclusivity that leads to prejudice, educational and societal. The excluded can quickly become 'the others'. And a belief in the 'otherness' of the 'others' is one of the bases which justifies hostility and ultimately, violence towards them.

6 The Celebration of Patriotic Death: The Teaching of Literature

Until relatively recently, the epicentre of Europe's literature and the basis of much elite education were the three great classical epics, *The Iliad* and *The Odyssey* of Homer and *The Aeneid* of Virgil. The most esteemed, *The Iliad,* retains its hold over the European imagination despite being seldom read today, save in translation. Apart from the questions raised by the concept of its centrality to a European culture determined and dominated by a North European sensibility - it is essentially a Mediterranean work - it also raises questions about the centrality of war to the collective imagination and the consequent need to celebrate it in school.

The hold of *The Iliad* over the literary imagination and its educational concomitants are profound. Great poetry it unquestionably is and central to its greatness is battle and its associated friendships. Man becomes a god in battle and the gods themselves take part, enjoying the bloodshed, all described in gruesome detail. Generations of schoolboys brought up on it as great literature also imbued many of its attitudes - to the joys of fighting, to the exaltation of killing, to glorious or cruel disgusting death in battle, to women as cherished inferiors. Ulysses, one of its heroes, is the hero of *The Iliad*'s sequel, *The Odyssey*. This epic is not all warfare but has violence enough, ending in a massacre of suitors that would do a Clint Eastwood Spaghetti Western proud.

As European states were formed, they appealed to this history. To be connected with these heroic events was to demonstrate the heroic nature of the state in question. Warriors fleeing from the sack of Troy were the founders of many states, perhaps the most famous being Aeneas, celebrated by the third great Classical epic, Virgil's *Aeneid*, a story of an heroic warrior, the founder of imperial Rome. For centuries, European poets attempted to write founding myth epics based on these classical models, Spenser's *Faerie Queen*, Milton's planned but unwritten *King Arthur*, the French *Chanson de Roland*, Spain's *El cantar de mio Cid*, Camões' *The Lusiads*. Shakespeare wrote plays influenced by the classics and also celebrated England's bloody and heroic past. It was no accident that Olivier's version of *Henry V* coincided with the Normandy invasion in the Second World War with its evocation of heroism in the face of overwhelming odds. In the North of Europe, a different tradition, that of the Norse myths was also plundered. The influence of these myths on Wagner is well known, as is their influence in turn on Hitler and National Socialism.

While fiction extolling and celebrating war is still produced and remains popular, other forms of popular media play their part, not least the cinema. In 1999, Boyd Farrow commented on the resurgence of interest in the Second World War by Hollywood, noting that in the last 12 months some 30 films with Nazi themes had entered production in Hollywood and the same number in Europe including a dozen in Germany (Farrow, 1999). (In passing, he also noted that in 1998, some 40 new books about Hitler had been published in the USA (Ibid).) It seems that as schools in Europe have moved away from using literature and other reading materials as support for militaristic jingoism, popular culture attempts to fill the gap. A recent example of this was the popularity of Spielberg's *Saving Private Ryan* made in 1998, a dramatic but at heart war comic re-enactment of the Normandy invasion.

But it is not as simple as that. Nationalistic literature has indeed left most of the classrooms in Europe. The humbug of the English poet Newbolt for example, '...what Englishman of fifty wouldn't far rather stop the shot himself than see the boys do it for him?' is thankfully no longer studied (Newbolt, 1981). But as new states continue to be formed, the literature of the new nation has to be asserted or re-asserted or simply invented or expropriated. Such literature does not have to be a celebration of heroic warfare, indeed it can be the opposite. The famous anti-war literature of the First World War (and to a lesser extent the Second World War) is a case in point. Students in Britain study Sassoon and Owen's poetry and modern fiction inspired by them like the novels of Pat Barker (1992: 1993; 1996) and in Germany, Remarque's *All Quiet on the Western Front* (Remarque, 1929). Just about every state has 'their' authors commenting on war. Thus, for example, students in Greece may study English speaking authors but are more likely to read Myrivilis's *Life in the Tomb* with its powerful account of the fighting in Northern Greece in the First World War (Myrivilis, 1987).

However, literature can make a powerful educational tool to explore the reasons for warfare and the means by which it could be avoided. This is not so much through the study of powerful anti-war novels and poems such as those mentioned above but through the study of literature that explores the relationships between people and their country and between that country and others. A supreme example of this is *Ulysses*, mainly written in exile during the First World War by the Irish writer James Joyce. *Ulysses* is a useful prism to re-examine the preoccupations of both this chapter and the book more generally. A useful starting point is with the secondary hero of the novel, Stephen Dedlus and one of Stephen's intellectual preoccupations, his 'Ineluctable modality of the visible' (Joyce, 1960, p. 45).

Why is *Ulysses* so important? Its publication in 1922, in the immediate aftermath of the First World War, was a major event in the creation of the postmodern or late modern period with which we continue to struggle in education as elsewhere. Picasso, Stravinsky and other European artists were trying to come to terms with the relativistic universe discovered by Einstein and the collapse of the European dominated world order and its Enlightenment Project in the aftermath of that war. In contemporary university literature courses throughout Europe, Joyce's claim to primacy is seldom questioned nowadays. *Ulysses* consistently appears in lists of 'great works' and the text continues to sell in large quantities throughout the English speaking world. It is also translated into many languages, no easy task. Yet his games with language and his subject matter seemed shocking to most of his contemporaries. *Ulysses* was considered 'unreadable' and also pornographic, a paradox that Joyce might have enjoyed. That was still broadly true in the 1950s and 1960s but is far less so today. The verbal plays are the staple of much of the mass media, its sexual explicitness routinely overtopped on television and film. Students can now move easily from the early works of Joyce to the complexities of *Ulysses* without too much of a jar. The stylistic revolution that he set in place is recognised not only as revolutionary, but also as a powerful example of contemporary style.

However, perhaps as important is the fact that the text of Ulysses reinforces the late modern notion of the social determination and construction of text. This impinges on all levels of intellectual enquiry. Other chapters in this book keep returning to the questioned authority of historical and other educational texts, especially as they relate to national events and affairs. Joyce goes further than just looking at content. There is a traditional educational perspective, exemplified perhaps by Duthie (Shakespeare, 1949) that the text is unitary, - that a definitive text not only can but should be established. As a later editor of the same text puts it:

> Until recently, most textual critics assumed that editors should establish a text that "will be as near to what Shakespeare wrote as ... it is

possible to get" (Fowkes in Shakespeare, 1997, quoting Duthie).

Generations of Shakespeare scholars have attempted this task: only now is it seen that this task is not only not possible, it is not even desirable. This recognition is well described in the latest Arden Shakespeare text of King Lear (Shakespeare, 1997, p. 117 et seq.), where R. A. Fowkes makes a powerful case for there being several texts of the play, all with a realistic claim to status. Furthermore, it is well known that authors, Joyce amongst them, constantly reworked their materials. Although later readers may think the earlier versions are better, for example Wordsworth's two versions of *The Prelude,* it is probably in all of us to think that age brings greater wisdom and that the enthusiasms of youth are better tempered with the experience of age. Or, less flatteringly, that one wishes to re-write one's personal history. The poet T. S. Eliot put it well:

> As one grows older one may become less dogmatic and pragmatical; but there is no assurance that one becomes wiser; and it is even likelier that one becomes less sensitive (Eliot, 1951, p. 8).

This plurality of texts may appear confusing at first. In fact it is liberating. There is the need to worry less about the so-called authenticity of a single text and concentrate on students' response to the particular text that they are reading. This is not to say that all texts of a given work have equal status, it is that scholarship can reveal a range of texts that have legitimisation in specified contexts. It also has powerful links with the ways in which we regard and organise society more generally. In other words, just as the idea of a single, frozen text does not fit the facts, neither does a fixed and frozen history of a state, its triumphs and its tragedies.

Literature, like good (and indeed bad or pernicious) writing in other humanistic traditions, can be carefully studied, perhaps re-read and re-read, bringing new insights on each reading. *Ulysses* is a wonderful example of this. To say it has 'a meaning' which can be worked out is a nonsense. In such a way, texts about one matter can give insights into others. An example of this in *Ulysses* is its insights into issues of ethnicity and nationalism, of the relationship between the English and the Irish that the novel provides, giving a further layering of meaning and illuminating afresh earlier readings, which, of course, still run alongside these newer ones. Perhaps the way into these readings is to go back into the novel looking at the nightmare of history that it reveals.

"'History'", Stephen said, "is a nightmare from which I am trying to awake.'" (Joyce, 1960, p. 42). Indeed, later in the book, Stephen asserts that it is a nightmare from which you never awake. It is perhaps a modern European curse. One of the readings we get from Ulysses is this profound interest in and puzzlement by history. Not only is the book a magnificent commentary on Irish history, it is a commentary on European history. The book examines the ways in which states have mythologised themselves through inventing their history, as Simon Sharma has demonstrated in relation to the Netherlands (Sharma, 1991). That such an invention can prove to be a nightmare is something that Joyce, an Irishman understood.

Two component parts of this nightmare that continues to haunt Europe are the concepts of blood and soil in relation to the state and nationality. They haunt it because there is no satisfactory way of relating modern states to the people who live in them. British nationality laws have tied themselves in knots in relation to these terms, because the main intention of immigration legislation has always been to keep out groups of people that the English fear, the Jews, Black people and many other ethnic minorities that are seen as physically different by the white majority. Most other European states have legislation with similar intentions. State identities have to be invented as was the case with Holland in the 17th century, England in the 18th, Italy in the 19th and with Hitler's concept of Germany in the 20th Century. Similar processes are currently taking place in the 21st century in the states formed after the collapse of Yugoslavia. Retelling this invention to the young is one of a state's education systems primary tasks.

The literature in the state language or languages is critical here too as was mentioned at the start of this chapter. There is a strong desire that that the state's history has an imaginative strand. This traditionally has meant the epic. For ancient Greece (and indeed for a certain type of European identity) it was Homer's *Iliad* and *Odyssey*, the latter being the inspiration for Joyce's Irish epic. The problem is that the epic tradition itself needs constant re-invention if it is to retain viability, loyalty and induce patriotism. As an example of this, with increasing devolution in Britain, it will be interesting to see if we have such a re-invention of English identity, a development of the 18th century creation so well described by Linda Colley (Colley, 1996).

Another current example is the national anthem or state's official song, sung during the last World Cup and also during Euro 2000 (The Guardian, 1998). Some European examples:

Land of hammers, with a rich future. (Austria)

Prosper, O country, in unbreakable unity. (Belgium)

... tell to the world
that a Croat loves his nation. (Croatia)

Against us the blood stained banner
Of tyranny is raised
The banner of tyranny is raised.
Hear in the fields, the roar
Of her fierce soldiers.
They come right into our arms
To slaughter our sons and our daughters. (France)

Bloom my German Fatherland. (Germany)

Italian brothers
Italy has awakened
She has wreathed her head
With the helmet of Scipio. (Italy)

True to the fatherland I remain until death. (The Netherlands)

Wake up Romanians ...
Now or never is the time for you to have a new fate
Which should command of even your cruel enemies. (Romania)

O Lord God arise
Scatter her enemies
And make them fall.
Confound their politics,
Frustrate their knavish tricks. (UK)

Let the traitor of the fatherland be damned. (Yugoslavia/Serbia)

Scotland, a nation not a state, has:

> O flower of Scotland
> When will we see your like again
> That fought and died for
> Your wee bit of hill and glen
> And stood against him
> Prince Edward's army
> And sent him homeward
> To think again.

Not exactly the words to calm xenophobic sentiments in Europe. And not exactly great poetry either. They are revealing about state sentiment however and they are taught in school in many cases. Indeed, as this book was being finalised, a debate was taking place in Russia because their national anthem did not have any words. Some will be created and no doubt taught in Russian schools, supporting attempts to produce patriotic Russians, many of whose parents remain bewildered by the loss of the Soviet Union.

In the case of Ireland, not in that World Cup and thus saved embarrassment, Mary Robinson, talking about concepts of the nation, central to debates about the 'new' Europe, denied the usefulness of such terms as blood and soil, claiming that the terms have little value in determining the sense of being Irish in relation to their world-wide dispersal (Robinson, 1995). In this, she was perhaps moving on from Joyce's hero Bloom's view that 'a nation is the same people living in the same place' (Joyce, 1960 p. 430), a view rejected by the bigoted citizen in the bar:

> -What is your nation if I may ask, says the
> citizen.
> -Ireland, says Bloom, I was born here, Ireland.
> The citizen said nothing only cleared the spit out
> of his gullet and, gob, he spat a Red bank oyster
> out of him right in the corner (Joyce, 1960, p.
> 430).

Bloom, the dual identity Irish Jew is before his time or rather, his time is reluctant to recognise him and his dualities. But Bloom's view well demonstrates the two sides of nationalism, the inclusive and the exclusive.

European states have usually adopted the latter but not always, not for Bloom, not for Mary Robinson, and not for Joyce's *Ulysses*.

Perhaps one reason for this is that Joyce wrote *Ulysses* in exile. Trieste was an unusual mixture of a city at the time he lived there. The First World War was fought while he was there and its consequences for the region in which Trieste was located were immense. It was a time of upheaval which he experienced almost from the inside. An outsider, nearly an insider but never quite accepted. An Irish exile, like many who had gone before him and many who would come after, it is not surprising that his greatest work is located in Dublin. So the 'other' was a concept firmly in his mind. The Jews in Europe, a Jew in Dublin, an Irishman in Trieste coming from a British ruled colonial state: the author and his book are almost emblematic.

It is not surprising therefore that Joyce's Dublin in *Ulysses* reflects upon the anti-Semitism that was common at the time across Europe. At several points in the book, it is made clear that Bloom the Irishman is not seen as such by his countrymen, friends and acquaintance. Indeed, the book reveals a strand of anti-Semitism in Dublin that continues to shock by the unrelenting ordinariness of its ubiquity. It is likely that Joyce saw parallels between the lot of the Irish and the Jews within a broader European context. Both groups were denigrated, even suborned by more powerful groups. The consequence of this for Jews is well known, less so for the Irish. Yet it is because the Irish continued until relatively recently to be a major migratory society in Europe, that there is a greater complexity of debate about nationhood, belonging, origins, country and hatred than is found in many other European literatures.

That complexity is reflected in the book. The complex relationships between the Irish themselves and their relationship with England and the English are a constant theme as they remain today, for example in the work of Seamus Heaney (Heaney, 1995) and the modern Irish historians.

All this relates to education, not least in the English speaking 'Isles' off the mainland of Europe (Davies, 1999). Both British and Irish schools need to re-examine the literature and the history that is taught. Indeed, history in English schools still largely ignores the history of its immediate neighbours. Ask a secondary school pupil in England to list three historical events in Wales. Scotland will get you *Braveheart*, Robert the Bruce and the spider and perhaps Macbeth. In relation to Ireland and Irish history however, the new wave of historians of Ireland explore some of the issues raised in *Ulysses* in a different form, but one that is equally useful to education.

Some examples may be helpful to indicate the wide range of scholarship that is now available. George Boyce and Alan O'Day's work demonstrates how the divisions within Ireland have effected Irish historiography in negative ways (Boyce and O'Day, 1996): Stephen Ellis has re-examined the views of the Tudor state towards its internal empire and the mutual distrust it engendered (Ellis, 1997): David Hempton demonstrates that the decline in a sense of Irishness amongst Ulster Protestants dates really from the Home Rule Crisis of 1885-1920, although there were rumblings earlier in the 19th century. His book explores the role religion had in determining Irish, Welsh, Scots, English and British identity. Following Linda Colley, he argues that Protestantism and anti-Catholicism are essential ingredients of 'British' identity even today, when churchgoing has all but gone in much of Britain. Despite this decline, cultural and communal identity can rest on past religious practice undisturbed by current religious ignorance. The beleaguered mentality that he identifies in Northern Ireland particularly, thus finds compromise weak and against sectarian values (Hempton, 1996). Finally, two more specialised books deserve mention. Thomas Bartlett and Keith Jeffrey's work on Irish military history is a revelation (Bartlett and Jeffrey, 1997) and Barry Cunliffe's recent work on the Celts is a fascinating account of a 'non-group' of people, a sort of fictitious proto-European. He argues that the modern view of a Celtic world is erroneous. The original Celts were located in France but there is no contemporary record of them in either the UK or Ireland, yet it has blanket term for a language group and an artistic style that may have been the product of a wide range of peoples (Cunliffe, 1997).

Thus, a national epic can do more than raise nationalistic pride. In Joyce there is the pride but it is coupled with an acute sense of where unbridled pride can lead. Which in a sense goes back to Milton's *Paradise Lost*. Milton had the sense to see that a national epic did not fit the state around him and chose what he saw as the greatest epic of them all. But as William Blake said, 'the Devil had the best tunes' and amongst the best bits of *Paradise Lost* are, needless to say, the battles. Indeed, the debt to *The Iliad* is clear, not least in Book 1 (the book most frequently studied in schools) when Satan reviews his army.

Joyce is part of the answer to the difficulty that schools in Europe have in relation to literature teaching. He is able to take the Homeric epic and reject the martial glory it personifies and retain those other aspects that are often overlooked. But *Ulysses* is not exactly a primary school reader so is not the answer as a text. One response might be for schools to eschew the study of nationalistic martial literature. But that is not the answer. It would mean little Shakespeare for a start. Most European literature of the last 500 years has been either about warfare and its consequences or love and quite frequently both together. It should be taught and indeed needs to be taught.

A key issue concerns the selection of the canon. If military epics are seen as keystones of national literature canons as embodied in school and university syllabuses, then these institutions are trapped into the reproduction of male heroics. Peace has its literature too. Joyce, discussed in this chapter, or the Owen poem quoted at the end of Chapter Four represent this theme. Furthermore, the unseen messages in all literature need to be explored and the militaristic and nationalist assumptions challenged. By better understanding a wider range of their literature, Europeans will be better able, perhaps, to curb their more nationalistic and militaristic tendencies, and to reinvigorate their love of and understanding of literature.

7 Channelling Violence: Youth Movements and Warfare

Militarism and youth movements: Scouts, Komsomol, Hitler Youth

If many school students think that teachers cease to exist at the end of the school day, perhaps being hung up in a cupboard by the headteacher to await the next teaching day; so many in the formal education system have little idea of what happens to their pupils and students in their out of school time. But the wider society has long been concerned with this issue, or, more specifically, the dominant groups in society have worried about the out of school behaviour of the children of the subordinate groups. The rise of mass education across Europe in the 19th century had moved young people from the discipline of the workplace to the more problematic discipline of the school during the day. It is important to remember that for many working class families compulsory schooling was a contested issue. The loss of the young person's wage and the imposition of state enforced social control were resisted in rural as well as urban areas. As well as sustained absenteeism, still a feature of urban schools, there were even school strikes (Goodenow, 1983; Grace, 1979). Nevertheless, if schools kept young people off the streets during the day, there was still a nagging concern as to what the same young people did outside of school hours, a concern often expressed in the phrase 'the Devil finds work for idle hands'. There were two main fears: the first was that the boys would fall into violent and criminal ways; the second was that the girls would simply 'fall'. In both cases, the moral and social fabric of society was threatened. At the last, the solution would be prison for the one, the mental hospital for the second.

To prevent this, there developed during the 19th and early 20th centuries various forms of youth movements, particularly in the cities. Some of the earliest in the UK were 'Boys' Companies', quasi-military units set up to repel a potential French invasion in the 1860s but retained after the scare was over as their social control value became better appreciated. However, most were religious, most famously in the Sunday School movement. However, the introduction of mass education with its concern for discipline, well illustrated in Grace's work (ibid) ran alongside the beginnings of nationalist imperialism in society and led to the formation of more militaristic youth organisations such as the Boys' Brigade and the Boy Scouts. In Britain, these and other similar organisations were a particularly significant manifestation of muscular Christianity and English, religified patriotism (Leoussi, 1998).

The Boy Scout movement deserves particular attention in the context of its role in the preparation of young people for war. Founded in 1907 by Sir Robert Baden-Powell, a strange military hero from the Boer war, a particularly prolonged and violent colonial episode, it stressed duty to God and the King. It was not an original idea, being based on two American youth movements, the Woodcraft Indians, founded in 1902 and the even earlier Sons of Daniel Boone, founded by Daniel Beard (Microsoft Corporation, 1994). In its American origins, the stress was on adventure and outdoor life, but the Boy Scout movement, while incorporating these features, added more militaristic elements such as military style uniforms, ranks, salutes and a form of medal system in badges and other symbolic regalia. There was even drill with long sticks as weapon substitutes. It clearly demonstrated the perception that without conscription, young British males needed some form of military preparation. Today, it is an international youth movement based in Geneva, with over 14 million members in over 117 states and it consciously plays down its more militaristic past. However, for much of the last century, while the Scout movement may have been a force for good, it has also been supporting and encouraging the masculine, military and xenophobic virtues.

The USSR founded its own Communist youth movements, particularly, the Young Pioneers and Komsomol (Hosking, 1992), both deeply influenced by the Scout movement. The purpose of these movements was political indoctrination and social control. The Komsomol was used to recruit suitable candidates into the Communist Party and thus into the ruling class. The role of the Komsomol in recruiting emergency workers - for instance to help with a harvest or build a metalworks - is more conspicuous than any explicitly military role. Although Stalin tried to use Komsomol members to infiltrate the Red Army in 1941, these attempts were resented by soldiers and largely unsuccessful. By the Gorbachov period, the Komsomol had become discredited and young people preferred the informal grouping of sports clubs and pop groups. Unlike the Scouts Komsomol and the Hitler Youth were arms of the state. Whilst the trappings of militarism are evident in Komsomol, they were less important than in the Hitler Youth or even the Scouts. The ideal of peaceful internationalism (whatever the record of colonialism and Russification) remained a feature of these movements at both sides of the Second World (Great Patriotic) War.

The most obviously militaristic of last century's youth movements were those founded by the Nazi party in Germany. Generically known as the

Hitler Youth, they had three functions: to control youth; to indoctrinate young people in loyalty to the party and particularly to the leader; to prepare boys for the rigours of the forthcoming war and girls for its sacrifices (Stackelberg, 1999). Membership of the Hitler Youth became compulsory in 1935, though the National Students' Association had already taken the lead in the book burning episodes of 1934. Militarism and racism were not incidental features of the Hitler Youth but rather central planks of its function. Camps, military drill, parades and vigilante patrols were all important activities. German nationalism and anti-Semitism were celebrated in story and song. Indeed, Hitler Youth groups played an active part in the persecution of Jewish citizens. And finally, as Russian troops crossed the German border, the Hitler Youth were actually organised into active military units.

It was probably in reaction to these excesses that youth provision after the Second World War took on a more social and anti-militaristic function. Although much provision was of the table tennis and discussion of our problems variety, military training for young people was maintained in a few countries, including Britain. Young people, again mainly young men, practice dressing up in military regalia and shouting and marching about in schoolyards. They go on adventure weekends to camp, play war games and experience the thrill of handling real military technology. At this stage they are not usually allowed to kill or maim anybody but they are initiated into the rituals (competitive camaraderie, social license) and discipline (obedience to authority, nationalism) of military behavior (Coulby, 2000b). Interestingly, this form of youth provision survives longest in elite educational institutions: in Britain in 1997, Combined Cadet Forces (CCF) operated still in 198 public and 45 state (mainly grammar) schools (Thomson, 1997).

However, the broader debate about violence and disaffected youth continues, particularly in relation to young men. With conscription declining across Europe due to the ending of the Cold War and the increasing specialisation of military forces, military training as a civic duty and a form of social re-enforcement has declined in importance. On the other hand, youth work has increased but its impact on disaffected youth is questionable. Hence, the occasional voices, usually from the right, for a return, if not to military service than to some form of organised youth movement like the Scouts. Indeed the British government in 1997 flew the kite of reintroducing CCFs to state schools and inner city areas. It was suggested that they would help children to have a sense of self and national pride as well as fostering team spirit, which would be good for team games. In supporting such an idea, Michael Portillo, the Minister of Defence, with the support of John Major, the Prime Minister, was quoted as saying 'The Armed Forces save lives. They don't lose them, and the young people will learn discipline and hard work too' (quoted in Thomson, 1997). As a footnote to this idea, it should be mentioned that both men refused to join their own school's CCF when they were at school. Neither was Portillo's suggestion a new idea. In 1914, the Rev J. E. Roscoe, in a book with the edifying and patriotic title *The Ethics of War, Spying and Compulsory Training*, quoted, with approval, a fellow cleric, the Rev Hugh Chapman:

> After thirty years spent in the slums, my profound conviction is that nothing will go half so far towards the prevention of pauperism, drink, sloth, and all its subsequent abominations as compulsory military training (Roscoe, 1915, p. 32).

If the 'smack of firm military discipline' has not lost its credibility, the reason is perhaps the powerful hold that nationalism and warfare still has for some people. Perhaps some understanding of this can be gained by looking more closely at the impact of the Scout movement on such values. Although the Scout Movement is not to be compared to the Hitler Youth, this militaristic emphasis is quite clear in the writing of the movement's founder, Lord Baden-Powell. It is also interestingly revealed in the writing of Rudyard Kipling, an enthusiastic and committed supporter of the Scout movement. Kipling's writings on the subject deserve further examination as they were so deeply influential and clearly retain some residual force.

Literature, racism and youth

In 1923, Rudyard Kipling published a book with the uplifting title *Land and Sea Tales for Scouts and Guides* (Kipling, 1923). It was the seasonal gift for the year, running through several printings in the run up to Christmas. The book is a fascinating insight into the forces that have helped shape our educational institutions, both formal and informal. It is easy to forget now just how widely read Kipling was. Macmillan, the publishers with the English rights, sold seven million copies of his books during his lifetime. Doubleday, the holder of the American rights, sold a further eight million (Carrington, 1970). All this was mainly before the advent of cheaper paperback books. However, if a modern reader opens Kipling's book expecting to find uplifting stories for Scouts and Guides, they are in for a surprise, or rather a series of surprises. The first is on the title page, which proudly states the author's rank in the Scouts (Commissioner). This is followed by a suitably Scouting-For-Boys poem on the virtues of keeping fit, with the rousing refrain:

Nations have passed away and left no traces
And history gives the naked cause of it -
One single, simple reason in all cases;
They fell because their people were not fit (Kipling, 1924, p. v).

Racist discourse had quickly appropriated Darwin's 'survival of the fittest' to equate suitability with muscularity, indeed with military and imperialist aggression. By the penultimate decade of the 19th century imperial aggression was being justified on the basis of 'Darwinian' fitness in terms of racial, athletic and military superiority (Young, 1994; Young, 1995). The importance of fitness having being established, the first story gets straight to the point, being entitled 'Winning the Victoria Cross'. At once, the tone is set by Kipling proudly claiming that 'Any rank of the English Army Navy, Reserve or Volunteer forces, from a duke to a negro, can wear on his left breast the little ugly bronze Maltese cross with the crowned lion on top' (Kipling, 1924, p. 3).

Apart from the casual racism (and sexism and snobbery) of 'from a duke to a negro', note how Kipling has conflated English not just with Britain but indeed with the whole Empire. The chapter continues in much the same manner. Although the ostensible theme is (male) soldierly bravery, there are other undercurrents. For example, the enemy is praised more when they also see fighting as a manly activity:

> The humour and the honour of fighting are by no means all on one side. A good many years ago there was a war in New Zealand against the Maoris, who, although they tortured prisoners and occasionally ate a man, liked fighting for its own sake (Kipling, 1924, p. 13).

Or, in what seems at first sight almost a bizarre linking, when the enemy appear to share the view that warfare is a form of sport:

> Before the Great War, England dealt with many different peoples, and, generally speaking, all of them, Zulu, Malay, Maori, Burman, Boer, the little hillsmen of the North-east Indian Frontier, Afreedi, Pathan, Biluch, the Arab of East Africa and the Sudanese of the North of Africa and the rest, played a thoroughly good game. For this we owe them many thanks. (Kipling, 1924, pp. 4-5).

The list has a chant like property, redolent of British Empire stamp collections and cigarette cards of Soldiers of the Empire. Triumphalist on the surface, it was and remains, racist in its impact. It is also part of a long history of 'Empire stereotyping', which continues to influence many British children's racist attitudes to this day. The main difference between then and today is the seemingly endless range of racist stereotypes available to the British at the height of Empire, a range well brought out in Thomas Steven's nursery poem, published in 1902.

Babes of the Empire A - Z : An Alphabet for Young England

Babes of the Empire where sun never sets
Yours is the manfullest banner unfurled!
Yours is the proudest of all alphabets
Babes of an Empire as wide as the world!

Follow the sun from the east to the west;
Follow the birds from the north to the south;
Peace be the law where your faith is confessed
Love be the gospel that lives in your mouth.

Babes of Great Britain from sea unto sea
Happy the land where your monarch has sway!
King of contentment, and Lord of the Free
Yours be an Empire that fades not away!

* * * *

A's an Australian, born in the bush
An A.l. ally, when it comes to a push;
He can ride, he can shoot; and his gun and his horse
Are the flower of our Empire's irregular force.

B is a baby once known as a Boer
He was troublesome then, but all troubles are o'er:
Now his trekking and wrecking and fighting are done
Britain welcomes in peace her recalcitrant son!

C's a Canadian, hardy and bold;
A warm-hearted baby who laughs at the cold
And the fields of his harvest, so golden and free
Fine food for the Empire from sea unto sea.

D is a Dervish from sunny Soudan;
He dances no more his eccentric can-can
But, trained to our manners, is eagerly fain
When Britain once calls him, to dance in her train.

E is an English babe, ready to take
The yoke of the world for humanity's sake
So that every one knows, be it dreary or bright
When it's England that leads him, the road must be right.

F's a Fijian, her hair like a mop;
Let others spin yarns, *she* can spin like a top!
Now she's winning her way to a place in our nation
By skipping from frenzy to civilization.

G is a Gurkha - a big little man -
With a lion-heart under his covering of tan
He's fond of his kukri, his gun and his rice
If the Empire requires him, it needn't call twice.

H is Hong-Kong, with a pig-tail yards long;
(They always wear pig-tails in distant Hong-Kong!)
Though he laughs, he's not laughed at; he's old and yet
new;
There'll be no 'Yellow Peril' while he is True Blue!

I is an Irish babe - sweet little Pat -
With shillelagh and shamrock to stick in his hat
He has fought in his time; now no truer friend's seen;
We can wear our own colours while he wears the green.

J is a Jew with a ringleted head
Who's up and about while the rest are in bed
He's first on the steamer to sell you his wares
And he'll never be missed but at dinner and prayers!

K is a sweet little, neat little Khan
Who lives in a country called Beluchistan;
His head sports a turban, which looks a bit vain
But it covers a thoroughly competent brain.

L is Labrador - wee Esquimaux
Who lives in an ice-house all covered with snow;
She has sealskin for jackets, with nothing to pay
And is pleased with a land where its night in the day!

M's a Masai baby, fierce, dark and strong -
Who steals neighbours' cattle and thinks it no wrong!
That's in East Africa, where they appear
To have manners and customs quite different from here.

N's a New Zealander, - Maori child, -
Who hides in the bush, which is lonely and wild
His life's like a gipsy's; he lives upon snails!
But he danced like a prince for the Princess of Wales!

O is an Orange River Colony coon
Who dances and sings by the light of the moon
She's a Kaffir by birth, but our language she knows
And she always gets blacker the bigger she grows!

P is a Parsee babe, born in Bombay
Who is sure to be wealthy as Croesus some day
For these cute little Parsees our merchants admire
And so copy their fashions, make coin and retire.

Q comes from Queensland, the land of the Queen
The cleverest riders that ever were seen!
With a whip and a gun and a swinging lassoo
They're as swift as the wind to the swift Kangaroo.

R is a Rajput, who's haughty and proud
And turns up his nose at the ignorant crowd;
The horse that he rides is as proud as his master -
He will curvet and prance, but he won't gallop faster!

S comes from Scotland, the land of the cake
He's a braw little laddie a soldier to make
And the sound of his bagpipes will draw us all forth
When he comes marching south to the 'Cock of the North'.

T's a Tasmanian. The land where she dwells
Is as full of ripe fruit as the sea's full of shells
It was once a dark prison, but now it's all free
And sends England sweet cargo's from over the sea.

U's from Uganda, all woolly and black;
His clothes are a belt round a shirt on his back
Now he's got a new railway from shore unto shore
And the lions skulk off when the red engines roar!

V's a Victorian! That's a good name!
Preserving our honoured Victoria's fame
And the land's like her memory, so I've been told
With its jewels for setting and heart of pure gold!

W's a Welsh babe. Don't look at her hat!
Though it's shaped like a witch's, she's nothing of that!
She trips off to market, too keen to be late
And she sings once a year at a strange sort of fete!

X is an extra babe; just what we need
To complete our strong Empire in will and in deed!
And we hope every year, as the centuries fade
More excellent extras will come to our aid.

Y is a Yukon, - a wee red papoose
In a snug blanket-coat, and smart moccasin shoes
He's a creature of summer, without any doubt
For in winter it's always too cold to go out.

Z is a Zulu, with fierce assagai;
Do you think he could hurt you? I'd rather not try!
But he won't, if he *could*, for our battles are o'er
And now we're all friends - Briton, Zulu and Boer!

Babes of the Empire, from A down to Z
Peace be the law where your banners unfurled!
Happy of heart and contented of head -
Babes of the Empire that governs the world!

The poem is given in full, not for any literary merit it may possess, but because it shows not just the range of racist lexicon that was available to Stevens but also the gender and militaristic stereotypes that were common at that time. Few of the Empire's babes are female, probably because the major attributes portrayed are warlike ones. These were the same stereotypes that were also influencing what Kipling was writing some twenty years later. And in both cases, the writing was a conscious effort to inculcate proper attitudes in the minds of young people. In Kipling's case it was young Scouts and Guides, although one has to look hard for any hint that Kipling had Guides in mind when writing the book, save for a rather weak poem on how good female nurses are at looking after male babies.

Kipling finishes the book with a fascinating essay on his school, the United Services College, founded in 1874 to prepare middle class boys for the Army and Navy Officer Entrance Examination. All schools, not only those with a specifically military purpose, certainly all boys' schools, took the links between academic work and sport (*mens sana* etc.) and between sport and warfare as given. Or at least, many of the teachers in such schools did. Kipling was clear about these links in relation to his own schooling, writing proudly of the school rugby team being victorious over the enemy, i.e. the opposing team. He was also clear that a real man's life lay with guns rather than books:

> A scholar may, as the Latin masters said, get more pleasure
> out of his life than an Army Officer, but only little children
> believe that a man's life is given him to decorate with
> pretty little things, as though it were a girl's room or a
> picture-screen (Kipling, 1924, p. 258).

This is a bit of a put down for any Girl Guide who had managed to plough through the book to this point: her role in life was presumably to get out the glue and paste some more pretty pictures of flowers onto the new folding screen.

Military training in elite institutions

A further matter relevant to this chapter is the way in which the military elite are selected and prepared by the educational system. If the Scout and other youth movements encouraged the military virtues for the working and lower middle class children, other institutions, such as that attended by Kipling, were created to prepare the military elite, the officer class.

Unfortunately for the other ranks, officer training was considered unnecessary for much of modern European history. Leadership in battle was seen as inherent if one was a male from the upper classes. The significant change in this view came in the two revolutionary societies of the late 18th century, France and the United States. In Napoleon's armies, talent was encouraged and was generally the basis for advancement. His foundation of the St Cyr military college as a *grande ecole* in Paris was evidence of this and by 1866 nearly half of all the *grandes ecoles* were military ones (12 out of 31), although a hundred years' later this had dropped to only 6 out of 48 (Vaughan, 1969). Most other European states gradually followed suit, although omitting the meritocratic selection principles. Even in France however, these military academies were mainly upper class institutions by the end of the century.

An interesting educational aspect of their work was that they were amongst the first higher educational institutions of engineering and technology. For example, the Royal Military Academy at Woolwich was founded as early as 1741 (Barnett, 1969). Although military science was taught, the main impact of such institutions was to divide the top military leadership from the increasingly university trained civilian political leadership. As Wilkinson (1969) noted, such training was both a homogenising process, making its products similar to one another, as well as being a distinguishing process, making this homogenous group quite different from other elite groups. Enthusiasm for military science was frowned on in such elite military educational establishments, other social skills, such as horsemanship being seen as more important. In such an educational environment, initiative was smothered and a conservative and ethnocentric world view taken for granted. As Corelli Barnett commented, the British officer corps after the Boer War debacle was 'rich in evidence of the connection between birth, wealth and ignorance' (Barnett, 1969, p. 195). Also, as armed forces were (and largely remain) of necessity not democratic but hierarchical institutions, support for democratic institutions is muted.

Such lack of knowledge and understanding of democratic institutions in those with a near monopoly of armed power has proved dangerous to democracy across Europe. Although the officer class has retreated from politics in most EU countries, it is a relatively recent event. For example, the armed forces in Portugal kept Salazar in power until he died and continued to play a key role in Portuguese politics until 1976. The military dictatorship in Greece was finally overthrown in 1974. As armed forces struggle for a clear role in an age of sub conventional and low intensity wars and peace keeping activities without a Cold War background, it appears that the military is moving more into the mainstream of society. Two indicators of this are the increasing acceptance of women and gays into the armed forces, policies that would have been unbelievable a few decades ago and the increasingly more democratic intake to military academies. As examples of this, St Cyr recruited more than half of its intake from outside traditional elites by 1966 and Sandhurst's proportion of entrants from public schools dropped from two thirds in 1891 to less than a quarter by 1961 (Barnett, 1969, p. 198).

If fears of military dictatorships have faded in Europe, the vexed issue of military education and training remains less clear. Although professional military education remains an elite activity, it, like the education and training for other ranks provided within the armed forces, is increasingly marginal to mainstream education. With conscription declining across Europe, this process looks set to continue. What remains is the issue of the value, if any, of military training or the inculcation of a military ethos for the majority of young people in schools and youth organisations. The issue is made more pressing by the continued disaffection of many young males in the cities of Europe. This social exclusion seems to defy most attempts at diminution. At such times, the danger of looking back to an imagined more disciplined past based on military training in schools and in youth work is clear. This is not just a condemnation of military education and training. The evidence suggests that it just does not work.

8   Avoiding the Potential for Warfare: War and Peace in Ukraine

Ukraine is a fascinating example of how the people of a state with a violent past can learn from it, and using education as a part of a process, attempt to avoid potential internal conflicts leading to violence. It does this in the context of being a 'new' state with all the consequences for nation building in education as elsewhere that this involves. As a result, like other new states in Europe, codifying or even inventing their own unitary past is a serious business and is a significant purpose of state education. In addition, international trends such as globalisation and its local variations and circumstances make this aspect of education an uneven and even politically dangerous process.

Like many other parts of the old USSR, Ukraine is less well known as an independent state, although it has a long (and contested) history. It is second only to Russia in size as a European state and has a population of some 52 million people, again large by European standards. Its neighbours are Belarus, Hungary, Moldova, Poland, Romania, Russia and Slovakia, all of which have a place in the new state's history. Indeed, its borders with its western neighbours form part of the new 'Lace Curtain' which is being built to keep Eastern Europeans out of the expanding EU (Hearat, 2000). Its capital, Ukrainian Kyiv rather than Russian Kiev, was the centre, from the 10th to 13th centuries of the first great Slav culture and state, Kievan Rus. Whether Russia or Ukraine is that state's descendent is still a matter of dispute. Owning the past can be as important as owning the present. As a consequence both Russia and Ukraine teach a conflicting history. The solution to the argument is probably to accept that Kievan Rus was effectively destroyed by the Mongols in 1237, the territory squabbled and fought over just about ever since and that neither and both can claim that history.

It is more as a borderland in the sense discussed in Chapter Two that Ukraine is particularly interesting. With so many frequently acquisitive neighbours and being at the eastern margin of Europe, Ukraine has always been a frontier land, a border, boundary and march land, which more powerful states have invaded or ruled for much of its history - Scandinavians, Lithuanians, Mongols, Cossacks, Poles, Russians, Turks, Swedes, Austrians and Germans. Making sense of this history and creating what is, to many intents and purposes, a new 'nation state' is a major test for Ukrainian education as well as the other institutions of the newly independent state.

Another point that impacts upon education and the themes of this book is that the history of the state has led to the considerable ethnic diversity that is both a strong feature and also one of the most threatening elements within it. Although the majority (nearly three-quarters) of the population are Ukrainians, their Ukrainian language was in decline until independence in 1991 as the Russian dominated Soviet Union encouraged the teaching of Russian rather than Ukrainian in the schools. As a result, Russian is still widely spoken, although Russians are less than a quarter of the population. There are also many other small minorities, particularly along Ukraine's borders, befitting its complex history. One of significance for this chapter is the Tatar minority who live mainly in the Crimean Autonomous Republic, as their status poses significant questions for the state education system and indeed, for the state itself.

Independence has meant that the Russian language is in clear decline as it has lost its primacy in most schools in the face of a determined effort by the new government to promote Ukrainian at the expense of Russian. This has not led to the sorts of issues as were found in seemingly similar situations discussed in Chapter Nine in relation to the former Soviet Balkan states. Avoiding confrontation that tips over into warfare may be best understood if something of the state's violent recent history is detailed.

Ukraine's history is fascinating but cannot be gone into in great detail here (but see Ascherson, 1996 and Reid, 1998 for popular accounts). It is important however in that because it has been so turbulent, it has led to a far more stable state than was ever expected on independence in 1991. This seeming paradox may be better understood by looking at the various periods of violence and warfare that decimated Ukraine in the last century,

The first period started in 1914 when many Ukrainians, some in the Austro-Hungarian Empire and others in the Russian Empire, were conscripted into opposing armies to spend years fighting one another. Ukrainian nationalism, which had never died under the years of imperial rule, despite attempts to destroy it, continued to excite the minds of many of the intellectual class, especially teachers. The influence of teachers is underlined by the Tsar's 1876 Edict of Ems, which forbade Ukrainian in schools, removed all Ukrainian language books from the schools and exiled many Ukrainian nationalist teachers into Great Russia. Despite such draconian measures, the Russians failed to kill the language, in schools as well as in the wider society. It had however set a precedent in that the Ukrainian language has remained a point of contention even up to the present with some Russians still asserting it is only a dialect of Russian.

The wave of nationalism and political change that started to sweep through the losing empires in 1917 did not pass by Ukraine. In March, 1917, a *Rada* or parliament was established in Kyiv. Following the October Revolution in Russia later in the year, Red Army troops moved into Ukraine and ignoring independence claims by the Ukranian *Rada*, re-established Moscow rule. In 1918, the German Army moved in as part of the Brest-Litovsk settlement, while at the same time, in the West of the country a short-lived Ukrainian Republic was declared in the Polish speaking Austro-Hungarian section in the dying days of that empire. This double history continued in the aftermath of the First World War.

The Wilsonian principle of self determination left Ukraine still divided (Boemeke et al. 1999). In the west, Polish nationalism took drastic expression. In the chaos of the war and its aftermath, what today would be called 'ethnic cleansing' led to 1.5 million Ukrainians being killed in the period 1914-21 and a 'plantation' of 200,000 Polish settlers being established in the west of Ukraine. In education the Ukrainian language and the study of Ukrainian history was yet again banned; this was the more poignant and ironic as the first chair in Ukrainian History had been established in 1894 at the Polish controlled university of Lviv in western Ukraine.

In Russian dominated Ukraine, the story was even worse. The 1917 collapse in Russia led to the long Civil War, mostly fought in Ukraine territory, itself at that time divided between Poland, Russia, Czechoslovakia and Romania. For three years, five armies fought in Ukraine - Red, White, Polish, Ukrainian and Allied (60,000 French troops) plus Cossack bands. All, save the Allies, attacked Jews and there were massacres, with anything between 50,000 and 200,000 being killed (Reid, 1998). It was one of the great 'hidden' wars in the history of the 20th century and one that even now causes problems for the teaching of history in the new state.

When peace was eventually restored, Ukraine entered into a modest golden age under Soviet Communism and Moscow rule. *Korenizatsiya*, the educational policy that encouraged the development of indigenous cultures and traditions in education and elsewhere, was implemented across the new Soviet Union. It was part of Lenin's policy towards the national minorities, although a more cynical perspective might suggest that such policies were essential if the old Russian Empire was to be kept together. In the schools, children were being taught that the old, oppressive capitalistic empires in the region were dead and that a new era of proletarian solidarity, of which they were to be the vanguard, was just beginning under the benign leadership of Lenin and the Union of Soviet Socialist Republics. Yet, despite the rhetoric, anti-Russian sentiment continued in the schools as elsewhere in the new Soviet Republic: so did anti-Semitism. A few years into a new Soviet education system, Lenin died and Stalin came to power.

To have had the attention of Stalin was bad enough. To have had Hitler as well was a disaster for the Ukraine. Their malign influence only finally ended with the death of Stalin. It was a period of more than thirty years of unprecedented horror. Comparisons in relation to such levels of war and violence are often without value but suffice to say that probably no European country suffered more during that period than did Ukraine. It reduced a country and an education system recovering from the First World War and the Civil War backwards to where it had been during the most disadvantaged periods in the past. Only after the death of Stalin was the education system and the society restored to levels it had known in the early 1920s.

The long disaster started shortly after Stalin came to power in 1928. By 1929, 'dekulakisation' - the 'abolition of the kulaks as a class' - commenced in Ukraine. As the breadbasket of the Soviet Union, Ukraine was a prime target for its associated collectivisation. In three years, 12 million Ukrainians were deported, most never to return. In 1930, the great political purges began, causing yet more suffering and deaths. In education, *korenizatsiya* was abolished, as it was alleged that such national educational elements accentuated national differences as against class solidarity and as such incited national enmities. In some contexts the argument may have merit but in this one it had none. Again, Russification was the implicit political and educational agenda. The position was made even worse during the Great Hunger between 1932 and 1933. In that period, some five million more Ukrainians died from hunger or 'exhaustion' as official documents of the time euphemistically described it (Conquest, 1970). The purges of 1937 to 1939 were a dreadful postscript. No numbers for Ukraine have been made available, but given the total Soviet estimate of one million killed and twelve million sent to the gulags, the numbers for Ukraine must have been considerable. (The scale of individual atrocities was staggering: as recently as the 1980s, a mass grave of some 200,000 people dating from this period was found at Bykivnya near Kyiv (Reid, 1998, p. 122).) For many surviving Ukrainians, the outbreak of the Second World War continued the horror.

In 1939, as part the Molotov-Ribbentrop pact, the Soviet Union gained part of Galicia that was always considered part of the Ukraine by them and by many Ukrainians living in Galicia. A young and ambitious Russian politician from western Ukraine, Nikita Khrushchev, organised by 'popular demand' the incorporation into the Ukrainian Socialist Republic of this new acquisition. (It was Khrushchev who gave Russian Crimea to the Ukraine in 1954, perhaps making him in some ironic sense the 'father to the nation'.) Less well known is that he organised the deportation of anything between 800,000 and 1.6 million people, 10-20% of the total population of this newly acquired territory in the two years before the German Army arrived in 1941. Few of them survived the war.

Even worse was what happened to the Ukranian Jews after the arrival of the Germans. Many Jews had remained behind in Ukraine after their arrival, mainly because they had nowhere to flee to at that time. Behind the army was the SS. When they left in 1943-44 most of the Jews, some 2,250,000 people, had been murdered. These included the famous Jewish communities of cities like Odessa (180,000 murdered) and Kyiv (175,000 murdered). Perhaps the most notorious atrocity was that written about by Yevgeny Yevtushenko in his poem on the massacre at Babii Yar (Yevtushenko, 1966). In the poem he also notes continuing Russian anti-Semitism, for the Nazis were helped by their Romanian allies and by a small numbers of anti-Semitic Russians and Ukrainians. Reid tells the harrowing story of how 'Shooting the Jews' became a popular children's game in some areas, such was the scale and ferocity of the extermination (Reid, 1998, p. 157). A further 1,750,00 Ukrainians were also killed in the carnage of those years. Hitler is said to have ordered that the only education Ukrainian children needed should be reduced 'to one sentence: "the capital of the Reich is Berlin"' (ibid. p. 158).

In 1944, the Red Army returned and the Crimean Tatar population, accused by Stalin of collaborating with the Germans, was quickly deported, an atrocity discussed in more detail later in this chapter. Many of the men had just returned from service in the Red Army. Stalin, mindful of his minorities, also incorporated Czech Ruthenia into the Ukraine SSR, where he could keep a closer eye on another group of potentially dissident Ukrainians (Weinberg, 1994, p. 778).

Post war re-construction was slow but was eased by the massive investment in the Crimea, the home of the Soviet Black Sea Fleet. The education system was rebuilt along the lines established in the 1930s and 1940s, forming the pattern that remained in place, with minor alterations, until the collapse of communism. It is a familiar system, well described by Nigel Grant and others (Lane, 1978, Grant, 1979). And despite the current dislike for all things Soviet, the educational system was becoming more effective in producing a well educated citizenry.

The impact of this long period of violence and warfare on the Ukraine, ending with Stalin's death, is clear. Nothing could be that bad again or should be allowed to be was the general view of many Ukranians. Although the rhetoric of communism remained, in education as elsewhere, real belief in it had gone for many Ukrainians. The education system of the early Soviet pioneers was elaborated and improved but the history that it taught and the values and visions of the future that it espoused were less firmly established. Marxist-Leninism had less power than Christianity in secular schools across the rest of Europe and the history of Ukraine as told by parents, grandparents and other friends and relatives bore little relation to that which was being taught in the schools. An education system of denial had been carefully erected throughout Ukraine as in the rest of the Soviet Union. Nowhere was this clearer than in the Autonomous Region of Crimea.

Ascherson's book (Ascherson, 1995) makes clear that the Crimea, although part of the Ukrainian state, has a long, separate and fascinating history and one central to Europe's vision of itself. As part of Lenin's strategy to hold the old Russian Empire together in the new USSR, Tatar Crimea was made an autonomous republic within the Russian SSR in 1921, thereby recognising the Tatars' long history in and control over that particular place. The Tatar language was recognised but Stalin, against the wishes of its users, forced the change from a Roman to a Cyrillic script, a change which still causes resentment amongst the language's users, despite changing back in 1997 (Nissman and Hill, 1997).

Table 1. The decline of the Crimean Tatar population, 1789 1993

Year	% of Tatars in Crimea
1783	83
1897	34
1937	21
1945	0
1989	1.5
1990	5
1993	10

Derived from Open Society Institute, (1996)

In 1941 the German army arrived in the Crimea. As described

earlier in this chapter, large and prosperous minority populations like the Jews, were wiped out by the Germans. 61,000 other people, mainly ethnic Germans, were also removed from the Crimea by them. (Most of the large German community in the Crimea had been internally exiled by Stalin in the face of the German attack.) In 1944, the Russians retook the Crimea. Stalin, wrongfully claiming widespread support for the Germans by the Tatars, 'abolished' the Tatar nation, removed its autonomous status and removed the Tartars off to Central Asia in a horrific deportation programme. Starting on 18 May 1944, 200,000-250,000 Crimean Tatars were sent into exile. The Tatars estimate this expulsion killed some 110,000, half the expelled: official Russian estimates admit to 45,000 between 1944-48 (Wilson, 1994). Wherever the truth lies, the expulsion was near-genocidal in its impact on the Tatars and was the last in a long line of Russian attacks on their nation (Kozlov, 1988), as Table 1 (above) illustrates.

With the removal of the Tatars, Russians were encouraged to immigrate and take their place in the new industries and services supporting the expanding Soviet Black Sea Fleet based at Sevastopol. In 1954, Nikita Krushchev made the Crimea a region of the Ukrainian SSR, which made geographic sense and was based on the apparently reasonable assumption of the continuation of the USSR. It was not a reasonable assumption.

The collapse of belief in the Soviet Union by Ukrainians was not a sudden affair but had a long pre-history rooted in warfare and violence of an intensity and length unusual in a modern European state. A series of post Second World War violent events are also significant: the invasions of Czechoslovakia, Poland and Afghanistan and the public unmasking of Stalin, particularly in his Ukrainian atrocities like the mass grave of Bykivnya. It was a violent but un-warlike event that was crucial as well. This was Chernobyl. On Friday 26th 1986, a nuclear power plant at Chernobyl, just north of Kyiv, virtually blew up. The Gorbachev-led USSR tried to cover up the disaster as did the local Ukrainian Communist Party; indeed, to this day, the full consequences of the explosion are still unclear. In Ukraine as in the rest of Europe, many thousands have died from the radiation and many more will continue to die from its consequences. In addition, some 150,000 people are still displaced in Ukraine as a result of the catastrophe (United Nations High Commissioner for Refugees in Ukraine, 1997). The nationalists in Ukraine, as the news came slowly out of the government information machine, found that this was the last straw. Western Ukraine had always been Ukrainian nationalist but this disaster spread the disillusion with Moscow rule across the whole of Ukraine. However, it must be said that Ukrainian nationalism really grew in response to the collapse of the Soviet Union rather than being a cause of the collapse. This relatively low-key nationalism has meant that the post-Independence Ukraine has not felt the need for a strong nationalist bias in its new post-Soviet curriculum. Also, as in Eastern Europe, the protests against the Soviet system started early but the collapse when it came in 1990-91, was relatively sudden and, thankfully, peaceful, which again helped to defuse extreme nationalism.

Indeed, it was the fear of such nationalism that led to the Ukranian Communist Party being in the forefront of the drive for independence. As the Soviet Union collapsed, the issue was fast becoming who was going to lead an independent Ukraine rather than whether or not it was to become independent. Leonid Kravchuk, a former Party ideologue, put the party's dilemma clearly before the decisive vote in the Rada. Speaking in Russian he said: 'Today we will vote for Ukrainian independence, because if we don't, we're in the shit' (Quoted in Reid, 1998, p.215). Hardly a heroic statement to be enshrined in school text books alongside the US Declaration of Independence or the French Tennis Court Oath.

The new state of Ukraine had two large areas that still saw themselves as rightfully belonging to the equally new Russian Federation, a peninsula, the Crimea, which was Russian speaking and Russia orientated as well as the eastern part of Ukraine which was similar (the Donbass). The new government in Kyiv had to tread a delicate path between the various nationalistic factions, nowhere more carefully than in the Crimea (Wilson, 1993). The changes following the collapse of the Soviet Union were made more complex in the Crimea by the return of many of the Crimean Tatars who had been expelled by Stalin. The Tatar population rapidly increased, from 38,000 in 1989 to some 260,000 in 1993 (Open Society Institute, 1996, p. 27). Now mainly speaking Russian - only half speak Tatar well (ibid.) - they returned to the Russian dominated and Russian speaking Crimea, wanting to re-assert their national identity and cultural 'ownership' of the peninsula. However, Ukrainian nationality law, based on international convention (Abdureshitov, 1996), initially excluded many Crimean Tatars from citizenship, as they were not resident in Ukraine on its gaining independence, as they were still in exile. Nor could they speak Ukrainian, an alternative criteria for citizenship (Fraction of Kurultaj of Crimean Tatar People, 1996). Work in state controlled enterprises is restricted to Ukrainian citizens and with privatisation of the economy of Crimea remaining underdeveloped, rates of unemployment among the Tatar remain extremely high (over 40%), despite them having high rates of educational qualification, acquired in their exile (Zubarev, 1996).

However, the Tatars were not crucial to the stability of the area. The population in the Crimea in 1997 consisted of between 60% and 65% Russians, 20% to 23% Ukrainians, 10% Tatars and 1% others, mainly Germans and groups from other parts of the former Soviet Union, especially the Caucasus states (Piskun, 1996). Nearly all are Russian speaking, even the Ukrainian minority. However, the new Ukrainian state insisted that the state language, and the language of instruction in Ukrainian schools, should be Ukrainian (Kiev Post, 1997). Yet the state had been mainly Russian speaking when it was part of the USSR and the language of instruction in the schools had been Russian. The scene was set for a dangerous confrontation over educational and other social provision which could easily lead to conflict and violence (Bremmer, 1994). It did not happen. Despite serious tension, violence was avoided. And with political stability has come educational stability.

A key element in this is the issue of the language of instruction. The Ukrainian state wants Ukrainian to be the language of instruction but is prepared to be flexible in areas where there are other large language groups. This is because only about 50% of 'Ukrainian' Ukrainians are really fluent in the language. However, for example, now 90% of first graders in Kyiv are in Ukrainian medium schools - while 76% of the adult population speak Russian - with clear evidence of the gradual Ukranianisation of everyday speech in Kyiv, despite its earlier low status. Russian/Ukrainian bilingual conversations are common and not seen as threatening (as is also the case in Catalonia but not in Quebec (Arel, 1996)). President Leonid Kravchuk in 1993 said:

> When we talk about bilingualism, it is always about the defence of one language - Russian: but I would like it to be about the defence of two languages, Ukrainian as well (Solchanyk, 1993. p. 3).

Data for the Crimea are not available but it is likely similar patterns of multilingual language use are increasing. The reasons according to David Laitin are threefold: firstly, economic return for changing to the state language, secondly, an appreciation of the loss of status of a previously high status group (the Russians) and thirdly the converse, namely the increase in status of a formerly low status group, viz. the Ukrainians (Laitin, 1996). Unlike the Baltic States, this change is taking place with a low level of acrimony. This is probably due to the lack of coercion and also due to the awareness of how conflict can destroy, as it has done for so long in Ukraine.

There are other educational issues. What history, what literature and what social education should be taught are also vexed questions. What influence should religion have in relation to education is another. The various groups within the Crimea, and across Ukraine more generally, have different aspirations and understandings. Coupled to that is the fact that the education system remains near to collapse due to chronic underfunding. Teachers are paid irregularly, the buildings are crumbling and new schemes to improve things have to cost nothing or be funded by external sources. But the system is slowly improving.

Other signs of improvement and of opposition to division are also apparent. In 1997, a new NGO programme 'Integration into Ukrainian Society of Crimean Tatars, Armenians, Bulgarians, Greeks and Germans formerly Deported from Ukraine' started, funded by the Soros Foundation. It indicated a willingness to co-operate between the various parties previously feuding over their position and status in the new Ukrainian state. Furthermore, in April 1997, national elections left President Leonid Kuchma and his party just short of absolute majority in parliamentary elections as left wing parties gained 42% of the vote. The Ukrainian nationalist parties were heavily defeated. Given that Ukraine now has a relatively stable economy and hyperinflation has gone, these are all signs that Crimea and Ukraine in general have passed through their previous dangerous uncertainty. The fears of internecine violence of the early 1990s have faded if not quite disappeared. But given that Ukraine was compared to Yugoslavia in terms of its explosive ethnic mixture, with the Crimea being the detonator, the Ukrainian state has to some extent defied expectations. For this, memories of the period under Stalin and Hitler must claim some credit. The horrors that extended over much of this century influenced most Ukrainian families. With increasing economic stability, the wish to plunge into ethnic conflict continues to diminish.

Other elements have helped in the stability of the new state. Communism has been rejected and the free market adopted with more or less enthusiasm according to an individual's market position. Political parties on democratic lines are evolving and maturing. It is, for example, unlikely that a party would repeat the famous (and truthful) slogan of the ultra-nationalist party in an early election 'vote for us and it is the last time you will have to vote' (Quoted in Reid, 1998, p. 298). The old party elite has realigned itself to new values without loosing too many of its former privileges. Modern Ukraine looks Westward rather than to the North. Membership of NATO and the EU is sought, not unrealistically, in the medium term. As Petro Mykolaiovich Talanchuk, the Minister of Education said in 1993: 'Now that we are not geared to the Soviet Union we have less need to manufacture products such as aircraft carriers' (MacGregor, 1993, p. 12).

Initial fights over language and cultural issues, at their most extreme in the Crimea, have gone underground if not faded away. The curriculum has been completely changed, rejecting the former Marxist-Leninist curriculum, although difficulties remain over the content of history and literature curricula. Ukraine's recent past and the position and role of the existing groups within the state remain a delicate subject. Ethnic Russian wishes to remain Russian and the Tatar dream of a homeland remain difficult educational as well as broader political issues. The education system is similar in certain respects to the one that it has replaced but the Ukrainian emphasis on gradualism and consent seems to be successful, As Cerych noted in the broader post Soviet context, educational systems like that of Ukraine face difficulties over:

- resource levels;
- the balance between decentralisation of education and the need to maintain state unity;
- the continuing need to find more appropriate curricula content;
- related initial and in-service education for teachers;
- perhaps most importantly, the drive to develop and maintain effective quality control systems (Cerych, 1997).

All this within the broad context of supporting national unity and nation building through the educational system. It is one of the good things that has emerged from a frightening history that Ukraine's education system has survived looking far more effective in meeting the educational needs of its citizenry than it was before 1991 as well as supporting unity and combating potentially lethal divisions.

9 Education and the Threat of Warfare: the Baltic States

The destruction of the Berlin Wall gave visible expression to the collapse of the Iron Curtain, the end of Soviet domination of Eastern Europe and the eventual reunification of Germany. Peace in Europe had broken out. However, sometimes the visible moments are themselves misleading. Romania was to wait several years after the demise of Ceausescu before the *securitates* relaxed their grip on power and the modernisation of the economy and the state could proceed. The elections in 2000 have again cast in doubt the commitment of the Romanian people and state to modernisation. Romanian nationalism, however, has now been decisively rejected.

In the period since the collapse of communism, the countries of the expanding European Union and the states of eastern Europe and the former Soviet Union have all undergone major transitions, in a not dissimilar fashion to the changes that swept Europe in 1945. And, as in the post 1945 period, dramatic political changes are matched with dramatic educational changes. Victory, over the fascists in 1945 or over communism in the 1990s, was followed by educational reforms based on a mix of economic and nationalistic policies that contain the seed of future violence within them. This chapter focuses on the changes in Eastern Europe and the manner in which educational reforms in this region have the potential to sustain violence, making a particular case of the Baltic states. It attempts briefly to identify and differentiate important features of these changes, some of which have potential for violence, and relates these to some of the concomitant changes within education systems.

As the book has constantly emphasised, Eastern Europe is a political and socially constructed term rather than a geographical one. Greece and Finland are actually further east than Poland or the Czech Republic. The continued use of the discourse of east and west may reflect the anachronistic, divisive thinking of the Cold War period but it also reflects a new version of the old fear - the invaders from the east. What is intended here is an analysis to cover the states of the former Soviet Union and some of those over which it had influence such as East Germany, Hungary, Czechoslovakia, Poland and Romania.

In eastern Europe features that characterise this transition from communism to the present state of affairs include:

- political freedom;
- economic liberalisation;
- nationalism;
- the breakdown of social order;
- a renewed interest in the west.

These matters are clearly linked and not all states display all these features. They constitute the generalisations within which individual examples can be identified.

The extent, or for that matter the benefits, of political freedom in these states must not be overstated. Whilst speech, publication, worship and media are certainly substantially freer in a great many states, from the Czech Republic to Estonia, there are many groups who would question the nature of their new-found freedom: Crimean Tatars, Russian speakers in Latvia, Chechens everywhere. Nevertheless, in many parts of eastern Europe, there is an exceedingly widespread awareness of a greatly enhanced perspective of personal freedom and renewed political participation. The former communist parties themselves have in many cases performed a miraculous transformation into electable democratic organisations.

This political liberalisation has been the accompaniment, if not the precondition, for economic liberalisation. With varying degrees of pain, the eastern European economies are being transformed to participate in the global market. The pain has been extreme in many cases: between 20% and 40% reductions in industrial output; mass unemployment at the same time as the social security net has been removed; the irresponsible introduction of unbridled free market economic policies which had already been strongly modified in the west (Pinder, 1998). Nevertheless, whilst massive inflows of international capital are still, in most states, eagerly awaited, a few economies are already on a clear convergence with their western neighbours, as is recognised by the planned admission of Estonia, Poland, the Czech Republic, Hungary and Slovenia (along with Cyprus and Malta) to the EU. (The status of Latvia's application is discussed in the final section.) A further tranche of east European countries plus Turkey are almost certain to follow.

Significantly, the admission of Poland and Estonia will give the EU (and already in the Polish case NATO) further land boundaries with Russia. The recent economic crisis in Russia, combined with the persistently worsening economic performance in countries such as Romania, indicates that not all states will be able to make a smooth change of economic system as that effected in, say, Hungary. Indeed, commentators in Romania have begun to question the notion of a 'transition' to a western style economy and society. More generally, without substantial internal reform and equally solid investment from the West, Bosnia-Herzegovina, Serbia, Bulgaria, Albania and Romania may not emerge to a future of economic liberalism and prosperity but rather remain trapped in post-communist conflict, bureaucracy and poverty. The lexicon of transition is however, inherently optimistic, that of a difficult period which can be passed through to happier times. It is then more obviously applicable to Estonia and Latvia, say than to Former Yugoslav Republic of Macedonia (FYROM) and Georgia.

Apart from applications to membership of the EU, the renewed interest in the west is also manifested in the expanded membership of the Council of Europe and the expansion of NATO. Tourism and commercial and educational visits have increased from east to west as well as from west to east. Western products and styles are much in demand. Western broadcasts can now be received across Eastern Europe and their popularity is all too often in inverse proportion to the quality of their content and the impartiality of their reporting.

This transition has not been without its downside. The breakdown of social order, the re-emergence of nationalism and the outbreak of actual war being among the three most notable aspects. Crime rates have exploded in Sofia as well as in Moscow and St Petersburg. Drug abuse and vandalism have accompanied Microsoft and Coca-Cola into Eastern Europe. The processes of privatisation have allowed for collaboration between *aparatchiks* of the previous regime with local and western criminal organisations to make huge, illegal and semi-legal fortunes at the public expense. Especially in Russia, organised crime, linked to the police and political structures, has become exceedingly prevalent (Castells, 1997; Castells, 1998).

Especially for the older generation, there is a widespread perception of a breakdown of social order that, along with the perceived tardiness of western financial commitment, provides much of the groundswell towards the refashioned communist parties. Those countries identified above as being more entrenched in poverty than emerging from any economic transition are also the ones that the western institutions, notably NATO and the EU, are most reluctant to accept. Progressive politicians in Romania, for example, have demanded economic change and sacrifice on the basis that it would lead to a successful application to join the EU (and associated economic paradise). When the application was turned down in 1998, there was a risk that extremist political parties, nationalist as well as communist, might benefit to the further detriment of economic and social progress.

The manifestations of re-emergent nationalism have varied from the citizenship laws of the Baltic states, discussed below, and the break-up of Czechoslovakia, to civil wars in Yugoslavia, Georgia and Chechnya (Cohen, 1996; Ignatieff, 1994; Pavkovic, 1997). This nationalism has highly particularistic loyalties and is capable of generating the most intense passions and violence. It is exacerbated by apparent economic disparities, between Slovenia and Serbia or between the Czech Republic and Slovakia. It constitutes a major threat to the stability of many parts of the region: currently including Kosovo, Macedonia (FYROM), Vojvodina and Bosnia. Furthermore Russian nationalism and its uneasy relationship with that of many of its new neighbours - the Baltic states, Georgia and Moldova - may also come to constitute a continental threat. If the period of transition in eastern Europe is not to be even more bloody, then some control over nationalist sentiments and activities as well as greater economic and political stability in Russia would appear to be essential.

Education in times of transition

These transitions in Eastern Europe, then, were associated with various levels of the democratisation of the central state and the attempt to involve it in the reintroduction of capitalist modes of production, distribution and consumption. In many states this engaged a rhetoric of restored freedom and national identity. In most states it involved a rejection of communism and of Russia/the Soviet Union. Property was redistributed from the state often to those who could claim to be the former owners. In this process much of the land and industrial capital actually came into the hands of the former party *aparatchiks*. This group maintained economic and often political power in some countries such as Romania. Elsewhere, as described for the Baltic states below, nationalist forces were sufficiently strong to break the *aparatchiks'* grip on wealth and power.

Just as states differ in the extent to which they are involved in the transitions described above, so they differ in the extent to which they seek to adapt their education systems to address these changing circumstances. Whilst there certainly are structural aspects to this adaptation - the emergence of private, selective and streamed institutions - it is on curricular aspects that this chapter particularly concentrates. To what extent have the curricular systems of eastern   European schools and universities been adapted to recognise and facilitate the wider transitions? This section of the chapter focuses on curricula and nation building and nationalism in Eastern Europe generally and the final sections take up the case of the Baltic states.

Education had not been the only instrument of Russification (Haarmann, 1995). Other, less subtle techniques had been used: mass murder, mass deportation, the influx of Russian speakers, party and citizenship restrictions on national language speakers. But language and educational language policy was a key element of Russification across the former Soviet Union. The Soviet approach to asymmetric bilingualism had been at best assimilationist, at worst the attempted destruction of nations such as the Inguchetians, the Chechens, the Volga Germans and the Crimea Tatars (Khazanov, 1995). National language speakers in the three Baltic states felt that their languages too had been taken to the edge of elimination. Language then was a critical area of nation building in many of the newly independent states. The transition was widely characterised by changes in national and educational language policy. In Estonia, Latvia and Lithuania, Russian ceased to be the language of many schools and is rapidly being replaced in the universities. The first foreign language in a great many states ceased to be Russian and became English or German.

Other important changes involved the abandonment of Marxist-Leninism as the paradigm discourse for a variety of subjects from sociology to biology in schools and universities across the former Soviet Union and eastern Europe. The transitional states rapidly used educational policy to redefine the nature of truth and error. History had to be fundamentally re-written and Soviet internationalism to be revealed as a further aspect of the centuries long expansion of the Muscovy state. 'In the former Soviet union,' the joke goes, 'the past is always unpredictable'. Across eastern Europe paragraphs on Soviet friendship and brotherhood were deleted from history and social sciences textbooks and replaced by ones on the suppression and ultimate triumph of the national destiny (Silova, 1996). Familial hatreds moved into the discourse of schools.

National culture, no longer in the shadow of the Moscow-controlled state culture machine, found itself with a central dimension in the curricula of schools. In Latvia, folk song and folk dance, manifestations of the rich national tradition, could take up the school time previously given over to dreary, polytechnical wishful thinking. Schools and universities were set free to celebrate the nation, to reinforce the strength of its language, to re-make its history and to re-shape its civil society. In Tajikistan the universities are introducing new courses in management, world culture, the history of religious ethics and ancient Tajik languages (Holdsworth, 1998). In this emancipatory, epistemological transformation, many states are still engaged, perhaps unaware of the nationalist sentiments they may be unleashing.

As the example of the Soviet Union itself indicates, nation-building and nationalism-building are all too often closely connected. In many newly independent states of the former Soviet Union, nation building took the form of the denigration of the Russian language and of Russia which too often had as its political accompaniment, harsh restrictions on citizenship (Lieven, 1993). In Eastern Europe too the re-writing of history and the celebration of culture focused on a narrow definition of what was the nation, who were the true citizens and who had been the historical enemies. The rediscovery of the nation and national identity was accompanied by a rediscovery or recreation of the other (Coulby, 1997b; Cucos, 1997; United Nations Development Programme, 1995). The Serbs reasserted their difference from Bosnians and Croatians; more peacefully the Slovaks established their distinctiveness. Russians and Chechens threw off the fiction of peaceful, Soviet internationalism. In Latvia, Russian speakers were stripped of their citizenship and many associated human rights. Latvia is only an extreme example here. The disenfranchisement of minorities is common across the region: The Czech Republic excludes gypsies and Slovaks from citizenship (Mazower, 1998). Of course, nationalism figures as a continuity as well as a transition. The treatment of Magyars and Gypsies in Romania was little improved in the new democracy from their conditions under the xenophobic Caeusescu regime.

In this reassertion of nationalism the schools and universities have played their part. A surprising number of the most outspoken Serbian nationalists were academics as manifest in the infamous memorandum of the Serbian Academy of Arts and Sciences (Mazower, 1998). In the invention of tradition, the school and university curricula stressed a particular view and period of history, the Battle of Kosovo, say or the 1939-45 period, which identified peoples of other languages, scripts or religions as potentially dangerous others; in extreme cases as enemies. In Bosnia-Herzegovina, Croatian children were actually taught in schools that President Tudjman of Croatia was their president and Croatia their country (Done, 1998). The textbooks were from Croatia and reinforced the message that they were a people unfairly denied union with their true state. The sense of solidarity invoked by literary masterpiece, folk song or common enjoyment of sacred landscape has too readily become a sense of solidarity against the other.

The shift to English as the second language is leading to the neglect of the other languages of the state and of near neighbours. The attempt in some cases such as Estonia has been spectacularly successful but internationalisation has been at the expense of a rejection of regional continuity. Neighbouring St Petersburg has the same population as Estonia and Latvia combined. And these five million people speak Russian. The unfortunate and, in some instances disastrous, concomitants of reawakened national identity have been revived xenophobia, language based politics and regional isolationism: a process in which school and university curricula have played a significant part. In some instances, such as Serbia (Rosandic, 1994) this has led to a curriculum potentially and actually destructive of democratic politics.

Linguistic nationalism and the potential for violence in the Baltic States

Distinctions between groups of peoples in the Baltic States are made on the basis of either religion or language. It is the latter distinction - in particular between Russian on the one hand and Latvian, Lithuanian or Estonian on the other - which forms the main focus of current politics. Language in this region is rather readily conflated with ethnicity. The transitional independent states have attempted to portray themselves as linguistic or ethnic nations (in this they reflect a more general trend described in Hobsbawm, 1987). It is possible that nowhere is the fallacy of the nation state more potentially dangerous than in Latvia, Lithuania and Estonia.

To understand this danger and the way in which it concerns education and citizenship in a period of transition it is necessary to have some knowledge of the history of the Baltic States during this century. The difficulty is that the interpretation and even the facts of this history remain deeply contested (Overy, 1998; Mazower, 1998). Following the peace treaties that ended the First World War, Lithuania, Latvia and Estonia became independent states. At this point their demographic profile was substantially different from what it was in 1991. In all three countries there was a significant Jewish population, with some cities being historically and demographically important components of the diaspora, such as Vilnius in Lithuania and Daugavpils in eastern Latvia. In all three countries, but especially in Latvia and Estonia, there were also significant Russian (speaking) minorities.

Their independence was betrayed by the Molotov-Ribbentrop Pact, during the Second World War the Baltic States were successively invaded by the Red Army, the *Wermacht* and the Soviets again. Baltic forces fought for both sides as well as for independence movements. This was a period of atrocities. Responsibilities for these remain contested. By the end of the war the Jewish population had been almost eliminated in local as well as distant death camps. The German population had largely fled westwards. In 1945, Lithuania, Latvia and Estonia became Soviet Republics. This was not the choice of their populations but, following the defeat of Germany, reflected the military power of the Soviet Union across eastern and central Europe at that date.

The period of Russification of the Baltic states between 1945 and 1991 involved demographic, economic, political and educational processes. Through waves of systematic purges, Lithuanian, Latvian and Estonian people were transported en masse to Central Asia and Siberia. Many who resisted Soviet incorporation were murdered. Others fled as refugees to the West. A parallel and opposite demographic movement of Russians into the Baltic States was implemented. This rested on the Soviet development of industrial facilities in the area and more particularly on the military installations rapidly established in the warm water Baltic ports. The demographic profile, especially of Latvia and Estonia, was radically transformed. In 1934 Estonians represented 88.2% of the population, in 1989 they were 61.5% (Estonian Institute, 1995). By 1993 Latvians represented only 54.2% of the population of the state (United Nations Development Programme, 1995), having been 75.5% at the high point of 1939 (Lieven, 1993). This demographic profile was most visible in the cities. In Daugavpils, to take an extreme example, out of a total population of over 120,000 in 1994, 56% are Russian, whilst Polish and Latvian speakers both represent about 15% (Multinational Culture's Centre, 1995): this probably underestimates the Russian population; Lieven (1993) gives 87% Russian speakers. Riga has 60% Russian speakers as against 30% Latvian. Tallinn has just over 50% Russian speakers (Lieven, 1993).

The economic processes were such that the Russians in the Baltic States during the Soviet period were often seen to have the best paid jobs, frequently in the military or security services. Political processes supported this: the newcomers were provided with new housing, while Latvians, for instance, subsisted in poor conditions. The politics of Soviet internationalism were actually, in the south and west as well as the north of the enlarged Soviet Union, those of the continuation of 18th and 19th century Russian expansionism. The Baltic States were Russified.

Education played a major part in this process. Schools and universities were adapted to the production of the ideal Soviet citizen. The history of the 20th century was accordingly rewritten - not for the first or the last time: its unpredictability has already been noted. The status of the Russian language became ever more important in schools and universities. Russian became the first language of many schools and of higher education. It became the second 'international' language of all other schools. Lithuanian, Latvian and Estonian, or for that matter Livonian, Polish and Ukrainian (the latter sometimes denied a linguistic status) did not have this status in the Russian speaking schools where English or German were more likely to be the foreign languages. Thus speakers of the Baltic languages spoke Russian but speakers of Russian did not speak the Baltic languages. Russian rapidly became the language of the military, of commerce and of education. Russian was the language of daily transaction in the cities - as indeed in many it still is. Educational institutions were used to implement policies of linguistic segregation and asymmetric bilingualism.

Dispersed and degraded, their language, their culture and their very 'people' seemed, especially to the Latvians and Estonians, to be being systematically wiped out. They were conscious of their history, as languages, cultures, independent states and major European trading cities, which went back many centuries. It was as if it were all about to disappear under the onslaught of Russification, disguised as Soviet internationalism. 'The Latvian nation was moving inexorably towards that point where national dissolution and extinction could become irreversible' (Driefelds, 1996, p. 50: though this source cannot be regarded as invariably impartial).

Given the current status of Russians, especially in Estonia and Latvia, given the actual history of the Jews in the Baltic states during the Second World War, the vociferousness and extremism of some Baltic nationalists may appear incongruous. Yet when the three states achieved independence, heralding the total dissolution of the Soviet Union, they had succeeded, from the point of view of many of the participants, in wresting political independence from the seeming brink of cultural ('ethnic') extinction. The education and citizenship laws that were rapidly put in place reflect this. Having nearly lost a cultural war, they were determined to win the next. It is to these laws and cultural wars that this chapter now turns.

Baltic education in transition

Laws were put in place so that in Latvia, Latvian is the one official language and in Estonia, Estonian was the official language. In both states only people who are literate in the official language were regarded as citizens by the law. People not regarded as citizens have no vote and cannot engage in political activity. (In Estonia non-citizens could vote in local elections only.) They carry a different passport from citizens and there are thus restrictions on their ability to travel. A large percentage of the populations of these countries thus suffer discrimination in terms of civic rights on the basis of their language. Furthermore, 'there have been changes in the Latvian labour law code permitting employers to lay off employees who cannot fulfil their professional duties due to lack of Latvian language knowledge' (United Nations Development Programme, 1995). The mass of 'non-citizens probably shun the naturalisation system because they regard the language and history tests as too demanding and at times even humiliating. This is contributing to a mistrust of institutions and reflects the psychological estrangement of non-citizens from the state' (United Nations *Latvia Human Development Report 1997*, cited in Vipotnik, 1998, p. 7).

The ability of people to learn a foreign language can thus determine their civil status. In this sense in Latvia and Estonia education and citizenship are vitally interconnected. To put it at its starkest: a Russian speaking pensioner, whose family have been living in Riga for many generations, who might have actively participated in the independence movement, now has to take a language examination before being eligible to vote. Not official policy in either state, though part of the political discourse in both, is the notion that Russians should go 'back' to Russia. Although Russia has said that it will accept any who proclaim themselves to be Russian, the current political and economic climate in that state is not one to encourage significant inward migration.

Educational policy in the region is now that characteristic of newly emergent or re-emergent states. The change in language policy is the most obvious. One asymmetric bilingualism has replaced another. Lithuanian, Latvian or Estonian have become the predominant language of schooling in Lithuania, Latvia and Estonia respectively (for a full description of language policy in Latvia see Kamenska, 1995). Attempts are also being made rapidly to shift the language of higher education away from Russian. 'The Baltic universities increasingly operate only in the Baltic languages, and quietly discriminate against Russian applicants' (Lieven, 1993, p. 314). Russian speaking schools continue, though their numbers are being reduced, and in these either Latvian or Estonian is the first and compulsory foreign language. The foreign language of Estonian or Latvian speaking schools is no longer Russian but German or predominantly English. Thus all young Latvians and Estonians will soon speak the official language but only some of them will speak Russian, the language of many cities and of the their neighbour, trading partner and major regional power. English is replacing Russian as the *lingua franca* between the three states in a denial of the regional geography.

All three Baltic states rapidly shifted their curricula away from the objective of creating ideal Soviet citizens. Their urgent concern was the invention or re-invention of a national culture. Great poets and artists, important scientific and technological developments, sacred landscapes and cityscapes are being discovered, re-discovered or, if necessary, invented. The history of each state, of its relations to the rest of the Europe and the wider world and of the various groups within the state are being rewritten. In this way a version of the state's importance, its culture, its identity and its history are being encapsulated within the school and university curriculum and thereby legitimated and reproduced to succeeding generations.

Religious education has been reintroduced as an optional subject in Estonia and Lithuania. The importance of Latvian and Estonian culture - in terms of folk music and dance - as well as in the discovery of a literary canon, is being stressed. Dance and music had been important components of the protected identities of groups, especially in Latvia during the Soviet period. This self-conscious identity indeed formed a part of the 'singing revolution' (Driefelds, 1996). Current and historic links with the West are emphasised in many activities: scientific, commercial, artistic, political. An official statement on education in Lithuania, for instance, stresses that 'The educational system is based on European cultural values... Educational reform is based on the educational experience of democratic Lithuania and Europe' (Lithuanian Ministry of Education, undated; see also Zuijine, 1995). This is another example of a seeming EU 'kite mark' of an appropriate education system, as is discussed in Chapter Ten in relation to Bosnia-Herzegovina.

The danger of these radical changes to school and university curricula is that these institutions are being involved in the encouragement of xenophobia as a mode of state building. This possibility is obviously attractive in newly re-emergent states. A sense of statehood may be encouraged by emphasising difference from other states, perhaps even distrust of the inhabitants of other states or a stress on their historical role in subordinating the 'true' citizens. The curricula of schools and universities implicitly or explicitly shift towards the encouragement of warfare in relation to the defence of the new state identity (Coulby, 1996). Such a temptation may be particularly attractive with regard to the state and inhabitants identified with previously colonising powers.

It seems almost as if there was an element of revenge in the policies pursued by politicians, otherwise enlightened, with regard to the Russian speakers in Latvia and Estonia. Combined with other policies on housing and on the payment of pensions to previous Soviet military and security personnel still resident in the two states, this may well be the perception of the Russian speaking people. And it may also be the perception of the much larger Russian population across the land borders within Russia itself. On the other hand, from the point of view of Latvian or Estonian speakers, these are essential steps to preserve the languages and cultures which Russification almost succeeded in eliminating and to redress the economic and civil wrongs of the Soviet era.

The politics of this region are important in European and indeed global terms. All three Baltic states are actively pursuing political and economic links with the West. As capitalist democracies with a long history of western links, and in close proximity to 'western' Finland, these connections are readily furthered. The Estonian currency has been successfully tied to the Deutchmark since shortly after independence. All three states wish to become members of the European Union (see below). They would furthermore welcome membership of NATO. In the medium term such developments would seem to be welcome to these western organisations. The Scandinavian countries in particular are keen to further their historical, geographical and commercial links with these 'new' Baltic states. They are also anxious to support all political developments that can assist in the establishment of stability and economic growth in the region.

At this point it is worth mentioning the dimensions of each of the three states in demographic terms. The population of Estonia in 1990 was little over 1.5 million (Estonian Institute, 1995); that of Latvia in 1993 was 2.6 million (United Nations Development Programme, 1995); that of Lithuania in 1989, 3.7 million (Lieven, 1993). Not one of them has as many people as, say, the adjacent city of St Petersburg. No matter what their success in transforming their economies, these states are unlikely to become world powers. They could not sustain the armed forces necessary to defend themselves against their militarily powerful neighbour. Russia has now almost completed its military withdrawal from the Baltic states though it maintains as its sovereign territory the naval base at Kaliningrad (Koenigsberg) on the Baltic coast between Poland and Lithuania. Russia is not the only post-Soviet nuclear power but it is unquestionably the main one. Events internally in Inguchetia and Chechnya, as well as externally in Georgia and Moldova, not to mention the confrontation with UK forces at Pristina airport in 1999, make it clear that Russia is still prepared to use conventional military power. These military interventions have been made by a moderate, ostensibly pro-western government. It is by no means clear that such an administration will continue in Moscow. The language and citizenship laws of the Baltic states, even without the actual or threatened expulsion of Russian speakers, is probably provocative to the people of Russia. It could certainly be made to seem to be so by any government with an expansionist eye on the Baltic ports and natural resources. These language and citizenship laws may become a source of regional and European instability.

It is notable that Lithuania has established a more positive foreign policy with regard to Moscow than the other two states. Legislators in Latvia and Estonia are faced with two sets of policy options. The first option is to abuse the civil rights of Russian speakers and to erode the importance and status of Russian as a language. This option depends on the continuation of Russian weakness in the area or on the almost certainly erroneous calculation that the existing and ever strengthening links with the west would be sufficient to deter any Russian military intervention or the threat of such. An even less realistic calculation would be that, were there to be any such intervention, the western powers in the shape of the EU or NATO would actively intervene. As western inaction against the ongoing state violence in Chechnya makes clear, it is one thing to intervene against states such as Iraq or Serbia quite another to risk war with Russia. The second option is to recognise that the economic collapse of Russia will not continue indefinitely; that Russia will remain a major trading power; that Russian speakers in the three states are an economic and cultural asset and should have equal civil rights; that educational policies and particularly language policies should recognise these issues of social justice and economic and political fact. As the Baltic states come to recognise the importance of Russia to their own trading position, opening up the Latvian port of Ventspils in preparation for Russian oil, for example, there are hopes that this latter policy may prevail.

Whilst, in the early years of regained independence, it was the first of these options that Latvia and Estonia followed, it is clear now that there has been an important policy shift in the case of both states. When all three applications were considered by the European Union, it was Estonia with its stable currency, its flourishing economy and its development of more progressive citizenship laws, which received approval to proceed to accession discussions. In the case of Latvia it was made clear that it was the citizenship laws which had prevented the state being considered for the first tranche of accession. This led to dramatic developments in 1998. A plebiscite of, largely Latvian speaking, citizens resulted in a vote to widen the franchise and to include Russian speakers as citizens. This move, supported by the government, has resulted in the position that Latvia will now proceed to accession discussions. It seems that a progressive attitude to diversity within the state and the move towards Europeanisation are inextricably linked. What remains to be seen is the extent to which the school and university curricula, having oscillated between two extremes, can now establish content which genuinely reflects the multilingual population and the geographical position and economic potential of the three states.

An ironic footnote to these nationalistic debates about citizenship is that they disenfranchise these states' potential military class. Many of the Russian families have long proud military traditions that they are more than happy to transfer to the new states. The states fear their loyalty and the overtures are rejected. Whether this is a vote for a pacific future or not is open to question.

This chapter and indeed this volume is an attempt to analyse processes which are far from completed. Certainly the expansion of NATO in 1999 to involve Poland, Hungary and the Czech Republic might symbolise that at least a stage in the process had been achieved. Elsewhere, further warfare in the former Yugoslavia and continued economic depression in Bulgaria and Romania question the very principle of post-communist transition: transition to what? What is clear is that the more simplistic assumptions embedded in the term transition - that Eastern Europe is in a period of being transformed into the likeness of Western Europe - must be rejected. The historical context is such that the political and educational actors do not see themselves as gaining independence, freedom, prosperity so much as *regaining* them. Their aspirations are no more towards western cosmopolitanism than towards Soviet internationalism: on the contrary they are towards a national self-consciousness embedded in language, culture and historical narrative as much as in political and economic institutions.

Indeed it is clear in these cases that education is not a consequence of political change; it is not a camp follower of the armies of transition. Rather it is an indispensable part of the process of transition and one of the institutions which is invariably involved in the process from the very outset. The transitions in Eastern Europe are ideological and epistemological just as much as they are political and economic. This was evident before 1989 in the attraction to western cultural forms and products from modern art to pornography and in the apparent resurgence of Catholicism in Poland and of Protestantism in East Germany. In the singing revolution of the Baltic states culture and language were both the mode and the goal of political contestation. The epistemological protocols that inform the school and university curricula in any state are important foundations of social control and reproduction. The educational transitions in Eastern Europe reveal the extent to which these protocols are profoundly contested and may not be taken for granted. They reveal further that this contestation is often dangerously predicated on nationalism. The hard lesson from Eastern Europe is that nationalism is far from a spent force. Its manifestations and self-perceptions are various - language, religion, 'ethnic identity', culture, historical narrative - but they are all latent within educational just as much as political processes. Nationalism is the bridge which links educational structures and knowledge on the one side to civil strife and warfare on the other.

10 Bosnia-Herzegovina: Warfare and the Re-definition of Education

This chapter takes some of the themes of the first section of the book to explain why education was unable to play a significant part in preventing the violence that took place as former Yugoslavia collapsed in the early 1990s. More importantly, this chapter looks at how the re-building of the system in one of the new states of the area, Bosnia-Herzegovina, is indicative of an implicit European Education Project, the vision of an effective, efficient and *peaceful* system. The war in former Yugoslavia has added that third aspect. Without it, effectiveness and efficiency would be the sole two aspects of educational reform and the dangers of further violence in Europe would be enhanced.

Education in the former Yugoslavia, efficient as it was, failed, as have many other European systems of education, partly because it failed to deal with the issues of nationalism and xenophobia raised in earlier chapters. Four issues in particular stand out in the Yugoslav case, all intertwined:

- the role in education of concepts of Europe and Europeans,
- nationalistic school and family histories,
- language in education issues,
- the place of religion in schooling.

When the collapse of Yugoslavia commenced Serbian militia leaders stated quite categorically that they were saving European civilisation and Christianity. The two clearly meant the same thing to the speakers. There is a temptation to think that statements like that tend to precede efforts to destroy what civilization there is in Europe and to commit acts that go against all Christian tenets. In this case they certainly did. The construction of the evil 'other' - the unfortunate Yugoslavians of Islamic heritage - took place in a dramatically short space of time. The hatred of Islam and the oppression of the Turks came back to life as if the events of the Ottoman Empire had taken place the previous month. In particular, revenge for losing the Battle of Kosovo Fields in 1389 was a real live aspiration for many Serbs involved in the violence. Indeed, some Serbian school textbooks deal with this defeat as if it were a victory (see Chapter Four).

Initially, Serbian fears were perhaps more about Croats than Muslims. Again this was a reliving of history, this time from the relatively more recent past of the conflicts of the Second World War, when the various partisan groups fought against each other as well as against the Germans. The more urban and educated elites had come to terms with this history but it still burned in many less urban parts of the state. After the relatively peaceful secession of Slovenia, the political leaders of both the Croats and the Serbs played on these nationalistic, atavistic fears and emotions and successfully provoked a war which they both felt they could win and benefit from, a process clearly delineated by Misha Glenny (1996; 1999). The former Yugoslav Republic of Bosnia and Herzegovina was to be neatly divided between the two. A lethal cocktail of misinformation about history, religion, geography and language fuelled a war that has been stopped but is not yet really ended.

The example of Mostar and its famous and symbolic old bridge illustrates this confusion well. A prosperous industrial town with a wonderful old central core based around the famous bridge, it was a mixed and increasingly inter-marrying community of Croats and mainly secular Muslims. The two groups fought together against the Serbs when they tried to take the town but when the Serbs left, the Croats attacked the Muslims and in the process wantonly destroyed much of the old town (Sells, 1996). It is now a divided town with no old bridge: where there was one university, there are now two, a Croatian one and a Muslim one. Each has TEMPUS and similar links with other universities across Europe. They have no links with one another. The city is divided into two non-communicating sectors and the schools do little to heal the divisions.

The Dayton Agreement has stopped the open warfare but has really only frozen the hostilities in place (Chandler, 2000). This compromise peace is supported by the international community in the hope that a range of social and political activities overseen by the United Nations through the Office of the High Representative (OHR), acting almost like a UN Trusteeship, will gradually bring about real peace and reconciliation in Mostar and throughout the whole of the new state of Bosnia-Herzegovina. Education is a key part in the process and a great deal of effort, thought and finance has gone into restoring education to make it play its part in the healing and stability process.

However, what is happening in education in Bosnia-Herzegovina is subtler than repair and reconciliation. It is no less than an experiment in bringing about an ideal European education system. The discredited former Yugoslav education system is to be replaced by an efficient, transparent, value for money, wealth creating, economy enhancing *and* peace sustaining system (Council of Europe, 1999). The last element is crucial. Without it, European intervention would have little more of value than the US economic interventions in Pinnochet's Chile. With it, the experiment, flawed as bits of it undoubtedly are, is a valuable attempt to make an educational system an active force for peace and reconciliation. In doing so, the model could be one to be reflected back on the rather smug donor systems in the rest of the world, particularly in the EU.

The experiment is needed as the peace process itself did little to restore or improve education. The Dayton Agreement of December 1995 created Bosnia and Herzegovina (BiH), a state with two *entities*: the Federation of Bosnia and Herzegovina (c. 75% Bosniak (i.e. Muslim) and 25% Croat, Serbs minimal) and the Republika Srpska (c. 95% Serbian). Crucially, education was devolved to the entities. Worse the Federation of Bosnia and Herzegovina has a ten canton Cantonal structure created by the 1994 Washington Agreements, implicitly based on a 'states' rights' perspective. The cantons each have devolved power over education, including higher education. Thus, education is administered in the Federation entity by a central Ministry without any real power and by ten cantonal ministries which have power but too little resources. In the Serbian entity, there is a central Ministry of Education, until recently indirectly controlled from Belgrade. In the Federation entity, all cantons have ministries of education with the full paraphernalia of educational government. One canton with 30,000 inhabitants thus has a complete national-type educational structure, down to wanting its own university. To further complicate matters, some of the cantons are 'mixed' cantons, with significant numbers of both Bosniaks and Croats. The wish of the Croats to have their own entity was denied them. In those mixed cantons there is often a dual rather than a mixed Ministry of Education with little communication between the two.

Faced with this complexity, donor countries have set up a series of supportive structures to help rebuild and transform the education system. Immediately after the war, there was a spate of capital programmes from donors to rebuild schools but little was given in terms of recurrent expenditure and money of itself could not replace the lost teachers and teacher trainers, either killed in the war or displaced as refugees. The wars had drained the society of much of its highly trained person power so that there was little left in the way of administrative support for the educational system either. Indeed, it has been said 'that by mid 1992 it was already no longer possible to speak of an education system in Bosnia-Herzegovina' (ICIS, 2000, p. 4). (There is an irony in that the highly educated people who left are not coming back, a stance tacitly supported by European donor countries who have a chronic skilled workforce shortage themselves and are glad to shelter well educated Bosnian refugees. The donor countries at the same time sponsor mainly unsuccessful repatriation projects.)

The main support process for education, is the 'Enhanced Graz Process', part of a broader 'Stability Pact' attempting to organise rational developments in the region. Six international working groups were set up in 1999 to look at what were seen as six key educational areas under two broad headings, peace and reconciliation strategies and strategies to bring about what might be called a 'European (more properly EU) standard of education'. The process has a double approach offering both resources now and in the long run potential EU membership.

Under the peace and reconciliation strategies were two strands,

- enhancing history teaching;
- enhancing education for democratic citizenship.

Under bringing about 'European standards of education' were the other four strands,

- enhancing vocational education and training;
- enhancing higher education;
- enhancing the non-formal education of young people;
- general educational system and policy improvement - the 'European standard'.

Of course all six strands cover both headings but the distinction is useful as it makes more explicit the role of education in preventing violence and bringing about reconciliation. However, what is interesting about these six areas is how they are perceived on the ground by educators.

A recent research study on these six strands for the EU found an almost universal understanding within Bosnia-Herzegovina of the carrot and stick approach (ICIS 2000). The carrot was welcomed, the stick often seen as unwelcome and even patronising. The six tasks identified by the Graz process for enhancing the quality of education also had uneven welcomes as the following brief description based on interviews undertaken with educational professionals in Bosnia-Herzegovina indicates.[1] The local responses to the value of each of the six strands also demonstrate their understanding of the close links between efficiency and equity which too often within the EU are seen as alternative educational policy outcomes.

i. enhancing history teaching. The outside experts rightly have identified nationalistic history as a key issue to be addressed: indeed, a major project on history teaching by the Council of Europe has a heavy involvement in this area. On the ground, however, it quickly became clear that it was too early to tackle this contentious area. Although history teaching was considered important by all people interviewed, the general feeling was that this was not a key (and indeed realistic) task at the current time because the nationalistic wounds were still open, albeit slowly closing. When there was a longer discussion of this subject, there was some enthusiasm for changing the *pedagogy* of history teaching, such as the introduction of evidence based analysis, but the *content* was still seen as contentious. However it was recognised that reform was necessary and that nationalistic and xenophobic history content should be changed. (One person's xenophobia is another person's patriotism.)

The OHR is still concerned by the nationalistic content of some textbooks used in the schools. This is not surprising as the Croat cantons mainly use Croatian textbooks while the Serbian entity uses books from Yugoslavia, which have a heavy Serbian bias. Censoring the textbooks by the OHR has been modestly successful but more remains to be done. Erasing offensive passages in existing textbooks only excited pupil interest and suspicion. One teacher, when asked by his students for the reason why the pages had been taken out responded: 'They have cut out our history'. It is an important issue. Textbooks can either confirm nationalistic and xenophobic myths or refute them. Research done in the former Yugoslavia suggests that the education system, excellent as it was in parts, did little to counter nationalistic myths (Pesic, 1994; Rosandic and Pesic, 1994, Stojanovic, 1994). However, it is important to realise that textbooks in most European states, especially history textbooks, are particularly vulnerable in this respect (Goalen, 1997; Pine 1997a and 1997b).

ii. enhancing education for democratic citizenship. The US Civitas programme is a large scale current project in the country. Based largely on US civic values, it is being seen as an improvement on what went on before. However, there was less enthusiasm for it than may have been expected. It was a classic case of inappropriate educational borrowing

---

[1] The following analysis is based on fieldwork notes made by one of the authors during the research rather than being based on the report.

and demonstrated that little has been learned from the imposition of one view of democratic education that occurred in relation to Germany and Japan after World War Two. On the ground, what was seen as important was the much more difficult task of changing the culture of teaching in both schools and universities to encourage a more democratic institutional mode as well as a more open approach to contentious issues in the teaching process.

   iii. enhancing vocational education and training (VET). Much is made across the EU of the importance of education for the knowledge economy and the successful development of human capital to support it. This is often at the expense of other aspects of education, such as its potential to support social peace and inclusion. Although the contribution of VET to knowledge economy building and economic development was understandably identified as a priority by both the Graz process and the World Bank report (Council of Europe, 1999), this was usually referred to obliquely in the interviews and was seldom mentioned unprompted. Despite this, the impression was gained that current vocational education and training was in a parlous state and that improvements needed to be made. The often expressed need for a better prepared workforce was accompanied by expressions of doubt and puzzlement as to in what manner and in what form such education should be put forward. Much of the traditional industry has been destroyed in the war and its restoration or replacement is problematic, particularly in a Europe deep into economic re-structuring. Improved vocational education and training then, while clearly seen as essential for economic and social development, remains a field where planning and development are needed.

   More specifically, reform is needed in the current educational provision at secondary level in relation to the obsolete vocational schools. Such specific reform would need to be seen as part of more general educational renewal, discussed in the sixth of the Graz's educational tasks (compare with vi below). There was also a perceived need in relation to higher level vocational education, discussed in the next section.

   In sum, the war had destroyed much of the existing industry and its simple replacement was not an option as much of it was un-competitive in the new free market conditions. Vocational education continued to educate for jobs that no longer existed, thus enhancing alienation amongst young people. As in other parts of Europe such alienated groups of young people can easily adopt nationalistic ideologies. In a state where such ideologies have still a purchase, the failure in current provision is serious. Whether there is an appropriate 'European standard' is open to question.

iv. enhancing higher education. Universities, like the schools, were badly effected by the war and rebuilding is slow. The Rectors and other senior university administrators and academics interviewed, naturally perhaps, saw higher education improvement as a crucial reform, making a contribution to both economic development and peace and stability.

Although there are already structures for information exchange at the Rector level on a trans-European basis, the interviews clearly indicated the need for assistance in a wide range of areas. These included quality assurance issues, issues relating to the change over from input to output models in terms of finance and graduate destination, curriculum renewal and the vexed issue of reform of university governance. In terms of internal cooperation, some progress has been made in following the recommendations of the World Bank report. However, for a sector devoted to the free exchange of knowledge, it was slower progress than might have been expected, particularly in relation to the fissured internal relations between universities serving differing national groups within the country.

Thus universities, often seen as bastions of free enquiry and disinterested scholarship, found themselves, often unwillingly, maintaining the divisions engendered by the war. This should not be surprising as universities and their staff were involved in the war and continue to face its consequences. Some are also in part engaged in the continuing quasi-nationalistic struggle as they work on critical curriculum reform areas such as language and history teaching. However, it would be unfair to assume that universities in the rest of Europe have completely overcome this issue as other parts of this book demonstrate.

v. enhancing the non-formal education of young people. This was seen as important but was never a top priority for any of the people interviewed. Whether this was because of the selection of people interviewed (mainly educational professionals) or it was genuinely not important was not clear. Perhaps it was a reflection of the more European wide disdain for youth work held by many working in education. It is a short sighted view. Youth work has access to many of the young people who have been relatively untouched by conventional education and as such, has a major part in combating nationalism and xenophobia amongst young people.

vi. general educational system and policy improvement. This is a catch-all category. In broad terms it refers to the reform of the educational system at all levels in order to bring it 'up' to a nominal EU standard or norm. Major elements in this are issues of effective management information systems, INSET for staff at all levels of the educational system, quality control/assurance systems and other aspects of the educational changes that have been implemented to a greater or lesser degree across the EU in the last decade. One key area from which the EU might learn in turn was the whole issue of the language of instruction. The development of Bosnian out of the old Serb-Croat is a modern example of how a new state asserts its unique identity in the light of oppositional linguistic facts.

What is exciting about these strands of reform is that they attempt to keep the aims of efficiency and equity in some form of balance. Efficiency, value for money, effectiveness are clearly the buzz words in education to assist in attaining EU membership. In a similar vein, most educationists in Bosnia-Herzegovina interviewed during this research believed in the healing and developing power of education in a state recovering from a vicious war. This was encouraging. Perhaps more worrying was the tacit view that education had had little or no role or part in the violent events that occurred during the war. Education clearly did not bring about the collapse of the former Yugoslavia. But it did less than it might have done to prevent this collapse. If there is to be an EU standard of education, the lessons from Bosnia-Herzegovina have much to teach.

11 The Victims We'd Rather Forget: Refugees in the Schools of Europe

This book started in Sarajevo. And indeed, former Yugoslavia has given much to the thinking behind the whole of it. Near the end, in a sense, the other end of an educational chain that started in Sarajevo ends. It focuses on a group of children in the schools of Europe who have often been the victims of warfare, ethnic cleansing and genocide. Children who have fled on their own or with families to the cities of Europe from Ethiopia, Indonesia, Rwanda, the former Yugoslavia and many dozen other countries. Refugee and asylum seeking children and young people are often the most recent and most visible 'others' in the schools and universities of Europe. They have unfortunately become the victims of the current manifestations of European xenophobia. Their treatment in schools shows the ways in which xenophobic violence can be institutionally mediated or reduced.

As Chapter Two indicated, Europe remains a difficult area to define accurately. Also, running through this book is the theme that deeply rooted in the European psyche is a belief that there are insiders and outsiders. The outsiders, whether European outsiders, national outsiders or both, are implicitly or explicitly identified to young people through the school curriculum. What this book demonstrates is that such stigmatisation is a foundation for violence and warfare that still seems to haunt Europe.

Of all groups of fallaciously feared outsiders in Europe, refugees and asylum seekers, are clearly the current favourites, seen as alien, to be shunned, feared and, it should not be forgotten, exploited. In the 1990s and 2000s, across the EU, refugees and asylum seekers have become the focus of that xenophobia which in previous decades had focussed on migrant workers and their families. Yet refugees are one of the largest 'peoples' in the world, 1 in 120 people globally being either displaced or a refugee. Even in Europe, where there are relatively few refugees compared to the rest of the world, there were, in 1997, 5,749,000 people of concern to the United Nations High Commissioner for Refugees (UNHCR), a number greater than the population of some European states, for example,

Denmark, Norway or Finland. And that large number was only a small part of the over 22 million people that concern the UNHCR globally (United Nations High Commissioner for Refugees, 1997).

Within the EU especially, asylum seekers are finding it increasingly difficult to achieve full refugee status, one of the (un)anticipated consequences of closer integration of immigration rules across the Union (Joint Council for the Welfare of Immigrants (JCWI), 1989) . The workings of the Schengen Group and the Steering Group on Immigration and Asylum are secretive and their findings subject to little public oversight. Indeed, the attitude of the Union and many of its citizens seems to be moving towards a view that most asylum seekers entering the Union are economic migrants abusing refugee procedures (Murdoch, 1997). The irony is that the demographic downturn in Europe will mean a need for millions of new immigrants to fill huge gaps in the workforce, anything up to 100 million by the half century by some estimates. Despite this, the current fears about migrants and asylum seekers continues unabated across the EU, encouraging the increasing involvement of criminals in the migration process. (A criminal cost/benefit analysis would show that smuggling people is more profitable and less risky than smuggling drugs.) Recent groups of asylum seekers like Roma from the Czech Republic fleeing systematic abuse and violence and Albanians seeking asylum in Greece and Italy have raised alarm rather than concern in the EU, leading to calls for further strengthening of the external boundaries of the EU (Mills, 1995). In particular, the non-EU borders of Poland and the Mediterranean coastline are causes for concern. As David Hearat commented:

> A new line of division is being carved through the heart
> of Europe. It will consist of wire fences, a force of border
> guards thousands strong and a network of watchtowers
> stretching 745 miles from the Carpathian Mountains in
> the south of Poland to the Baltic in the North... It is
> called the Lace Curtain (Hearat, 2000, p. 16).

However, a policy of fortress EU Europe (itself a suitably military term) is both unethical and unworkable. The lessons of the DMZ in Vietnam, the Rio Grande and the Berlin Wall do not seem to have been learned by EU policy makers. People desperate to leave will leave. Asylum seekers (and indeed economic migrants) will continue to arrive in the EU legally or otherwise, just as they always have done, fleeing violence and seeking safety.

Of course it is not just an issue for the EU. The CIS and the states of former Eastern Europe also have asylum seekers and refugees, mostly unnoticed by the rest of Europe. As the United Nations High Commissioner for Refugees commented in relation to the break up of the Soviet Union:

> It is one of the largest mass migrations in modern history. Since the break up of the Soviet Union, as many as nine million people have been on the move at any one time within the successor states of the Commonwealth of Independent States (United Nations High Commissioner for Refugees, 1997, p. 18).

For example, in Ukraine, the UNHCR arrived in March 1994 to help deal with a massive movement of people consequent upon the collapse of the USSR. (Some aspects of this were discussed earlier in Chapter Eight.) Since 1991, 1.4 million people have arrived from other parts of former USSR and 1.1 million have left for other parts of the former USSR; 300,000 more have left to non-CIS states, mainly Jews and Germans and there are 150,000 people still displaced by the Chernobyl disaster. On top of this, there are a few thousand asylum seekers from the rest of the world. The UNHCR had just $2 million to deal with this range of issues in 1997, a mere $68,000 of which was spent on education, as more basic needs had to be met (United Nations High Commissioner for Refugees in Ukraine, 1997).

So despite any humanitarian rhetoric of care for refugees, little is actually done for them. This needs some examination before looking at ways in which they may be better served. Why do people in practice not really like refugees and asylum seekers? The answer partly lies in their origins as the ultimate outsiders. Given the importance of state identity in Europe, to be without one is to be an outcast, with all the connotations, Biblical and otherwise, of that term. If they are non-white, they also have all the usual racism directed at them that their economic migrant peers and their descendants have.

State policies, educational and otherwise, to deal with such issues are inadequate across Europe, as they generally are everywhere. It is hardly surprising that large numbers of refugees perform unsuccessfully in schools and universities across Europe (Council of Europe, 1995). Many are poor and, in addition, face a new education system that makes few concessions to their needs, social or intellectual. In addition, they frequently belong to groups that are more generally socially marginalised or excluded. Where they do succeed, and numbers of them do, it is for a range of reasons, located in educational practice and/or in specific personal, familial or communal practices and attributes (Jones, 1993).

It is important to stress here the complex nature of educational success. Although success in public examinations is seen as critically important by all concerned, such evidence may conceal other issues. Students with equal examination scores may have very different access to the labour market or higher education. Immigrant and refugee students frequently need to have better results than those of many other students if they are to beat incipient or even overt hostility and discrimination. Girls and young women pose even more complex issues. Across Europe, there is growing evidence that girls are increasingly outperforming boys within the schooling system in terms of public examination results. This is educational success of course. But girls are still being tracked in terms of curriculum choice, particularly as they go up through the system. As a result, gender socialisation, in school and outside, remains sexist in many subtle and less subtle ways. Racism and sexism in schools, as well as particular religious and communal expectations on the part of the family, can combine to make the education of refugee girls particularly precarious. In a similar way, for an asylum seeking or refugee student, educational success is a combination of good scholastic results *and* good post school outcomes, if one is not to confuse the means with the end.

Current EU states' concern for output measurement in their schools may appear to have improved the lot of such students. General system improvement, for instance measured by public examination results, is on an upward trend in many EU states. The educational systems are improving. But general system improvement can often conceal the continuing educational failure of groups like refugee children as has been clearly shown by the work of Gillborn and Youdell, looking at English schools (Gillborn and Youdell, 2000).

Other aspects of educational success for refugees are more difficult to tie down. Monica Alvi captures some of this complexity in her poem *Exile*, about a young Bosnian refugee child in an English school (Alvi in Smith and Benson, 1993, p121). These two stanzas make the contrasts starkly clear:

> Try your classmates with
> the English version of your name.
> Maria. Try it.
> Good afternoon. How are you?
>
> I am fine. Your country -

you see it in a drop of water.
The last lesson they taught you there
was how to use a gun.

The child begins to feel safe and to enjoy schooling through the care of her teachers. And that is real educational success. Feeling confident, feeling safe, becoming at ease with oneself are important achievements to which schooling can contribute. Although teachers can do little in regard to broader societal practices, in relation to their own educational practice they can do much. A Kurdish refugee student (he went to university) identifies both the obstacles and the supporting factors (quoted in Rutter, 1997, p. 196). His account is worth quoting at length as it gives such a clear picture of the impact of school on a young refugee:

> Nobody wanted to sit next to me in lessons and no one wanted to have me as their partner in PE *(Physical Education)*. I was all alone in the corner. I did not understand the jokes during the lessons. I couldn't understand the subjects we studied because of my English and could never express myself during any simple discussion. I was too scared to talk because I knew if I made a mistake some of them would laugh at me. Once I even got beaten up by a group of students who used to bully everyone. They beat me up one evening when I was walking home alone. They said they couldn't stand me because I was a refugee who lived on the Government's money (which they considered to be their own money). After this I lost all my confidence ... I almost gave up. The reason that I didn't was because of my mother's help and the support I got from my teachers and a school charity.

As the extract details, he almost gave up but the combination of a range of supportive school and familial factors finally ensured success. Such individual stories are not uncommon and useful lessons can be learned from them. However, in order to do this, a range of contextual issues that affect the education of refugees and asylum seekers should be briefly considered.

Paramount here is the issue of legal status. Despite the UN Convention and EU agreements, actual practice in member states of the EU varies greatly. For example, in Denmark, asylum-seekers may be granted Convention refugee status or Danish *de facto* refugee status: the rights conferred to those granted Convention and *de facto* status are in fact equal. (In addition, a small number of asylum-seekers may be granted temporary humanitarian residence that has to be renewed at intervals.) Some 28% of all asylum-seekers were awarded Convention or *de facto* refugee status in 1995, while only 7% of asylum-seekers were rejected. In Germany, in the same year, of those receiving decisions on their cases, some 8.5% were grated refugee status, 2.5% *Duldung*, (tolerated residence permit) and 59% were rejected. Another 28% of asylum applications were not progressed, a common delay in many EU states (data from International Centre for Intercultural Studies (ICIS), 1997).

Uncertainty as to status, often linked with uncertainty about housing, health and financial support makes for a forbidding background to schooling (Carey-Wood et al. 1995). Against this links with other members of the particular refugee community are an important sustaining factor. Coping strategies are crucial to come to terms with the stress, even trauma, of becoming a refugee. This latter point cannot be over-estimated. Jill Rutter used Mona Maksoud's work with Lebanese refugee children to emphasise this, indicating that some 90% of this group of refugee children had experienced armed conflict, 50% had seen extremely violent acts including murder, 26% had lost family and friends and over 20% had been separated from their families (Rutter, 1998, pp. 24-25).

These are all important contributory factors to educational success. However, what happens in schools is crucial. At a recent EU seminar held in London to discuss refugee education issues, some common specific educational concerns were discussed (International Centre for Intercultural Studies (ICIS), 1997). Four areas in particular were seen as important, namely:

- Formal curriculum access issues, mainly relating to learning the language of instruction;
- Informal curriculum access issues, mainly relating to being the victim of racist or xenophobic bullying;
- supporting and validating asylum seekers and refugees prior experience, whether of previous education or the experiences involved in becoming an asylum seeker;
- providing appropriate initial teacher education and training (ITET) and in-service education and training (INSET) to teachers.

The chapter now considers each of these four points in more detail.

Formal curriculum access issues, mainly relating to learning the language of instruction. Although most EU states provide specialist help in relation to learning the language of instruction, no state has sufficient teachers expert in this area. Furthermore, it is an issue for all teachers, especially those working in large urban centres where the majority of young refugee students are attending school and college. Thus, helping students access the curriculum language is an essential part of initial teacher education, seldom the case in most EU states at present.

Related to this issue is that of supporting the first and/or community language of refugee school students. This is in the same dire position as bilingual education for minorities generally throughout the EU (Reid, 1997). What is happening in response to this is a rise in the number of supplementary schools or classes run by refugee communities, rarely with outside financial support. Like other supplementary schools run by minority groups in the cities of Europe, there has been little communication between the compulsory state sector and this particular aspect of the voluntary private sector. Yet there is much that the two can learn from one another, particularly in relation to refugees.

Two examples might be helpful here. The first is that while undertaking research in a primary school in relation to refugee education issues in London, it emerged that there was a Vietnamese Saturday school actually taking place in the mainstream school. Despite sharing premises and children, the mainstream school teachers knew nothing of the supplementary school (Miller, 1994). The second is that there are more of these schools/classes across the cities of Europe than many in mainstream education in the individual states realise. All give valuable support to the children's learning. They do this despite being funded by those who are amongst the poorest members of the community. Do the schools that are concerned about their refugee children have links with these schools? Do they know that they exist? Teachers and others in both systems have much that they can learn from each other. These and similar questions are far more than an expressions of concern about the value of communication and exchange. For if two groups of teachers teach the same children and teach them contradictory messages, as is possible, this is hardly in the child's best interests. However, even if the two systems just aim for better communication, there is much that can be learned and done.

A final point in respect of the provision of alternative education is the extent to which such supplementary schools and classes maintain not just old identities but also old enmities. The same question should, of course, also be asked of the mainstream curriculum. Children, refugees and non-refugees, may be taught that refugees are the product of war and violence but the causes of such wars and violence are rarely explored. Another opportunity to give young people a better understanding of the nature of warfare and of violence is still too often ignored.

Informal curriculum access issues, mainly relating to being the victim of racist or xenophobic bullying. Across Europe, as was mentioned earlier, there is an apparent fear of being 'swamped' by 'bogus' asylum seekers. On occasion this has led to serious violence, such as the murder of ten asylum seekers in a fire in Germany in 1996, a fire initially blamed on other asylum seekers rather than xenophobic German youth (Staunton, 1998). This unfounded fear of many non-refugee Europeans is reflected in schools, where many refugees, especially if they are not white, face hostility from some of the other, more established pupils (Jones and Rutter, 1998). The recent EU European Year Against Racism put money into a great number of anti-racist projects across the Union, some specific to refugees, but like many similar national initiatives, the results are unclear, as little public evaluation has so far taken place. Also the sums of money were relatively small and the profile rather than the purpose of the supported projects seemed more significant. More importantly, this latter point refers to a common criticism of work in this field, namely that good practice is generally poorly disseminated.

Particularly worrying is the ease with which negative stereotypes about certain groups of refugees spread across Europe. A current case is the negative views held of Kosovan Albanians. Long regarded in a negative light by many of their southern European neighbours, the negative stereotype of Albanians has spread to Germany, the UK and many other north-western European states and to many of the schools in those states. Some of the hostility links in with their supposed religious beliefs, the anti-Turkish/Muslim feelings which have such deep European roots and which the school systems of Europe do far too little to address. The fact that some have a Catholic background is either unknown or ignored. Nuances and stereotypes have little in common. Even if the Albanian refugee presence becomes accepted, as is likely to happen as the community settles and becomes less obvious as a victim of stigmatisation and social exclusion, no doubt another groups of refugees will take their place and also become the victims of such negative educational and other social processes.

Supporting and validating asylum seekers and refugees' prior experience, whether of previous education or the experiences involved in becoming an asylum seeker. Refugee students come into the classroom with a set of powerful previous experiences, particularly but not exclusively relating to the process of becoming a refugee. A teacher from a London school (Heillbronn, 1998), visiting a refugee camp noted the coming together of violence and education that is a common experience to many refugees prior to their arrival in the EU:

On alleys where they chased a fighter
white dusk hangs
We stumble on his bulldozed house
the rubble of a family's shatterings....

The children of the stones, said with pride
at warriors with crayons
making brightly coloured pictures
where stars tumble, people lie
matchsticks in pools of orange light.

It takes real teaching skill to help young refugees make sense of such a range of experiences. For example, Paul, a young refugee from the Republic of Congo, after skilful support from specialist teachers, wrote (Bolloten and Spafford, 1998, pp. 117-118) what was to all intents and purposes a 'found' prose poem on his own experiences:

Sometime I go in the tree ... and someone soldiers and they do get me, they push me and then they push me and then tree ... and I'm dead ... I go strong ... and then ... sometimes I go home I sleep my bed... and then...*(inaudible)* ... when I close my door I see my ... *(inaudible)* ... flower ... it's lovely flowers.

This writing is reflecting confidence in the learning environment that the young child was in and shows an increasing coming to terms with what must have been extremely traumatic experiences. Skilful teaching and support is crucial to this. Sadly, such skill remains in short supply and the schools systems generally do little to help young refugees come to terms with the violence in their recent history. Also, as mentioned earlier, their experiences, if handled with sensitivity and supported by other work across the curriculum, could be a valuable resource for tackling issues of conflict and conflict resolution more generally in schools.

  Providing appropriate ITET and INSET to teachers. Initial teacher training and education is already overcrowded in most European states. Of all the issues relating to refugees, the one most likely to be incorporated into initial training is adequate work on supporting bilingual students in mainstream classes. All European systems work on the assumption that children attend school having access to the state's language(s) of instruction. In the major cities, this is frequently not the case, yet little notice is taken of this in initial training. An interesting exception to this is the work undertaken by George Marcou in Athens: although the group he has been dealing with are mainly non-Greek speaking Pontic returnees rather then refugees, there are important lessons to be learnt from his work with ITET students (Markou, 1997).

Another important area of ITET is helping new teachers deal with racism and xenophobia and their potential for engendering violence. This is again an issue that effects more than refugee and asylum seeking students. This aspect of teacher education is rarely done well, although isolated pockets of excellence demonstrate that it is possible (Antonouris, 1995; Dragonas et al. 1996; Lahdenpera, 1996). In England and Wales such issues have long been excluded from teacher education. The arrival of New Labour has led to a belated initiative (Teacher Training Agency, 2000). However, this does not carry the force of statute so that those teacher educators who would wish to incorporate it in their programmes find that the weight of statutory material leaves them no time to do so.

In-service education and training (INSET) may be a more valuable area, as it can target teachers more accurately. Also, co-operation with other relevant agencies is an issue that can readily be dealt with in INSET sessions, although realisation in practice may well be more difficult. As well as dealing with issues that have already been mentioned, like language support and anti-racism, INSET is needed in the area of meeting refugee children's emotional and psychological needs, particularly in relation to trauma (Yule, 1998). It is also needed in relation to helping teachers deal with difficult and contentious issues like those around the area of conflict resolution.

Although the focus of these four points has been on the EU, they could usefully apply across Europe. Sadly, where there is most need, there is usually least money available for education generally and refugee education in particular, as the earlier Ukrainian example showed. But the discussion also shows that it is not simply a matter of resources but as much one of attitude. Of attitudes towards the needs of young refugees by educational administrators, teachers and the peers of the refugee and asylum seeking students. Such a change can take place. A school in London that works successfully with refugee students is Hampstead School. In writing about refugee students, Ruth Heilbronn (Heilbronn, 1997, p. 104) quotes a student teacher, learning to teach in the school:

> There are over 150 refugee students at Hampstead School
> and nearly a third of these are unaccompanied. This
> means that they have no family with them. A young boy
> of 13 fled from his country with a 'family friend' i.e.
> someone whom the family paid to take the child to a safe

place. He was dumped in the middle of the night at Islington underground station. He was alone in a country miles from his own land, having witnessed the most horrendous events, and the government told him he must go to school and study the national curriculum just like every other child. But he is not like every other child. How can education be important to refugee students when they have barely escaped with their lives? How can we as teachers educate them, make them feel welcome, try to help them through their trauma? The simple answer is that we cannot easily do so.

Such examples have encouraged the school to put in place a whole range of strategies, relating to the four issues identified earlier in this chapter. The result has been that the refugee students have adapted well to their new educational environment, with many of them reaching their full educational potential. An example of the school's success is given by this 18 year old Albanian refugee's story (again, she went to university), (quoted in McDonald, 1998, p. 157):

First we were like completely strangers but after a week we were part of the school. It was something strange to come to this school because before nobody came to the sixth form who couldn't speak English. Everybody helped. It was to them very interesting, it was strange - so they all rushed to help. Everybody was saying - "Do you understand? Do you want any help?" The teachers, too, were very nice - "Do you understand? Do you understand?" I know I was lucky. What I liked most was being friendly, trying to help. It was a big support because you feel stranger, like a total stranger in this place - and when you feel confident like nobody hates you and nobody is taking you as some kind of alien, so you just get free and speak yourself.

Schools indeed can make a difference to the futures of refugee and asylum seeking young people. As importantly, if schools make efforts to recognise and meet the specific needs of refugees, all children will learn more about the nature and consequences of violence. Refugees in European schools are a visible and constant embodiment of the place that warfare plays in our lives. Their experiences are a timely reminder to all school children and their teachers that the peace to which we have become accustomed in the EU is not just fragile but atypical in European and global terms.

Bibliography

Abdureshitov, N. (1996), 'Principles of restoration of citizenship in the former Soviet States.', in Chubarov, E. (ed.), *Citizen: Information Bulletin # 1 - 2*, 'Assistance' - Foundation on Naturalization and Human Rights, Simferopol, Crimea, Ukraine, pp. 12 - 15.

Allison, G. T. and Nicolaidis, K. (eds.) (1997), *The Greek Paradox: Promise vs, Performance*. Cambridge, Massachusetts: MIT Press.

Anderson, B. (1991), *Imagined Communities*. Verso, London.

Anderson, M. S. (1988), *War and Society in Europe of the Old Regime. War and European Society*. Best, G. (ed.) Surron Publishing, Stroud.

Antonouris, G. (1995), 'An "intercultural Europe" approach to the school curriculum in one teacher education institution', *European Journal of Intercultural Studies* 6, 3-12.

Appadurai, A. (1990), 'Disjuncture and Difference in the Global Cultural Economy', in Featherstone, M. (ed.), *Global Culture: Nationalism, Globalisation and Modernity. A Theory, (Culture and Society Special Issue)*, Sage, London.

Archer, B. (1997), '"A low key affair": memories of civilian internment in the Far East, 1942-45', in Evans, M. and Lunn, K. (eds.), *War and Memory in the Twentieth Century*, Berg, Oxford.

Archer, M. (1979), *Social Origins of Educational Systems*. Sage Publications Ltd. London and Beverley Hills.

Arel, D. (1996), 'A lurking cascade of assimilation in Kiev?', *Post-Soviet Affairs* 12, 73-90.

Ascherson, N. (1995), 'Afterword: Landscape after the Battle', in Britt, D. Ades, D. Benton, T. et al. (eds.), *Art and Power: Europe under the Dictators 1930 - 45*, Hayward Gallery, London.

Ascherson, N. (1995), *Black Sea: the Birthplace of Civilisation and Barbarism*. Vintage, London.

Bacon, F. (1937), *The Essayes of Francis Lord. Verulam*. Oxford University Press, London.

Baker, P. and Eversley, J. (1999), *Multilingual Capital*. Battlebridge Publications, London.

Barker, P. (1992), *Regeneration*. Penguin, Harmondsworth.

Barker, P. (1993), *The Eye in the Door*. Penguin, Harmondsworth.

Barker, P. (1996), *The Ghost Road*. Penguin, Harmondsworth.

Barnett, C. (1969), 'The education of military elites', in Wilkinson, R. (ed.), *Governing Elites: Studies in Training and Selection*, Oxford University Press, New York.

Barnett, C. (1986), *The Audit of War: The Illusion and Reality of Britain as a Great Nation*. Macmillan, London.

Bartlett, T. and Jeffrey, K. (eds.) (1997), *A Military History of Ireland*. Cambridge: Cambridge University Press.

Bash, L. and Coulby, D. (1989), *The Education Reform Act: Competition and Control*. Cassell, London.

Bash, L. Coulby, D. and Jones, C. (1985), *Urban Schooling: Theory and Practice*. Holt, Rinehart and Winston, London.

Bauman, Z. (1989), *Modernity and the Holocaust*. Methuen, London.

Baumann, Z. (1992), *Intimations of Postmodernity*. Routledge, London.

Bayley, J. (1981 (1963)), 'But for Beaumont Hamel...', in Hibberd, D. (ed.), *Poetry of the First World War*, Macmillan, London.

Best, G. (1998), *War and Society in Revolutionary Europe 1770-1870*. War and European Society. Best, G. (ed.) Sutton Publishing, Stroud.

Bhabha, H. (ed.) (1990), *Nation and Narration*. London: Routledge.

Black, J. (1997), *Maps and History: Constructing Images of the Past*. Yale University Press, London.

Black, J. (1998), *War and the World: Military Power and the Fate of Continents, 1450 - 2000*. Yale University Press, London.

Blunden, E. (1928), *Undertones of War*. Richard Cobden-Sanderson, London.

Boemeke, M. Chickering, R. and Forster, S. (eds.) (1999), *Anticipating Total War: the German and American Experience 1871 - 1914*. Cambridge: Cambridge University Press/German Historical Institute.

Boemeke, M. Feldman, G. and Glaser, E. (eds.) (1999), *The Treaty of Versailles: A Reassessment After 75 Years*. Cambridge: Cambridge University Press.

Bolloten, B. and Spafford, T. (1998), 'Supporting refugee children in East London primary schools.', in Jones, C. and Rutter, J. (eds.), *Refugee Education: Mapping the Field*, Trentham Books, Stoke-on-Trent, pp. 107-124.

Bowles, S. and Gintis, H. (1976), *Schooling in Capitalist America*. Routledge and Kegan Paul, London.

Boyce, D. G. and O'Day, A. (eds.) (1996), *The Making of Modern Irish History: Revisionism and the Revisionist Controversy*. London: Routledge.

Braudel, F. (1985), *Civilisation and Capitalism 15th to 18th Century. The Perspective of the World*, 3. Collins, London.

Braudel, F. (1989), *The Identity of France: Volume 1. History and Environment.* Fontana, London.

Bremmer, I. (1994), 'The politics of ethnicity: Russians in the new Ukraine', *Europe-Asia Studies*, pp. 261-283.

Bridge, A. (1993), 'Romanians vent old hatreds', *The Independent*, 19.10.93, p. 13.

Brubaker, R. (1995), 'National minorities, nationalizing states and external national homelands in the new Europe', *Daedalus* 124, 107-132.

Byrne, G. and Mckeown, P. (1998), 'Schooling, the Churches and the State in Northern Ireland: a continuing tension', *Research papers in education: Policy and Practice* 13, 319-339.

Caforio, G. (ed.) (1998), *The Sociology of the Military.* Vol. 11. The International Library of Critical Writings in Sociology. Edited by Newby, H., 13 vols. Cheltenham: Edward Elgar.

Cannadine, J. (1995), 'This skeptical isle', *The Times Higher Educational Supplement*, 24.11.95, pp.17-18.

Carey-Wood, J. Duke, K. Karn, V, et al. (1995), *The Settlement of Refugees in Britain.* Home Office Research Study No. 141. HMSO, London.

Carrington, C. (1970), *Rudyard Kipling: His Life and Work.* Penguin, Harmondsworth.

Castells, M. (1989), *The Informational City: Information Technology, Economic Restructuring and the Urban-Regional Process.* Blackwell, Oxford.

Castells, M. (1996), *The Information Age: Economy, Society and Culture: The Rise of the Network Society*, 1. Blackwell, Oxford.

Castells, M. (1997), *The Information Age: Economy, Society and Culture: The Power of Identity*, 2. Blackwell, Oxford.

Castells, M. (1998), *The Information Age: Economy, Society and Culture. End of Millennium*, 3. Blackwell, Oxford.

Cerych, J. (1995), 'Educational reforms in Central and Eastern Europe', *European Journal of Education* 30, 423-435.

Chandler, D. (2000), *Bosnia: Faking Democracy After Dayton.* Second ed. Pluto Press, London.

Chitty, C. (1989), *Towards A New Education System: The Victory of the New Right.* Falmer, London.

Clyde, R. (1996), *From Rebel to Hero: the Image of the Highlander, 1745 - 1830.* Tuckwell Press, London.

Cohen, P. J. (1996), *Ending the War and Securing the Peace in Former Yugoslavia*. Mestrovic, S. G. (ed.).

Colley, L. (1996), *Britons: Forging the Nation, 1707 – 1837*, Vintage, London.

Conquest, R. (1970), *The Nation Killers: the Soviet Deportation of Nationalities*. Macmillan, New York, NY.

Constas, D. and Stavrou, G. S. (eds.) (1995), *Greece Prepares for the Twenty-first Century*. Baltimore: John Hopkins University Press.

Coulby, D. (1996), 'Ethnocentricity, Postmodernity and European Curricular Systems', *European Journal of Teacher Education 18*, 143-154.

Coulby, D. (1997a), 'European curricula, xenophobia and warfare', *Comparative Education 33*, 29-42.

Coulby, D. (1997b), 'Language and citizenship in Latvia, Lithuania and Estonia: education and the brinks of warfare', *European Journal of Intercultural Studies 82*.

Coulby, D. (2000a), *Greek Civilisation as Curricular Construct: UK*, in *Comparative Education Society in Europe Conference: The emergence of the 'Knowledge society': from clerici vagantes to the Internet*, Bologna.

Coulby, D. (2000b), *Beyond the National Curriculum: Curricular Centralism and Cultural Diversity in Europe and the USA*, Falmer, London.

Coulby, D. and Bash, L. (1991), *Contradiction and Conflict: the 1988 Education Act in Action*, London Cassell.

Coulby, D. and Jones, C. (1995), *Postmodernity and European Education Systems: Cultural Diversity and Centralist Knowledge*. Trentham Books, Stoke-on-Trent.

Coulby, D. and Jones, C. (1996), 'Postmodernity, Education and European Identities', *Comparative Education and Postmodernity: Comparative Education Special Number 18, 32*, 171-184.

Coulby, J. and Coulby, D. (1995), 'Pupil Participation in the Social and Educational Processes of a Primary School', in Garner, P. and Sandow, S. (eds.), *Advocacy, Self-Advocacy and Special Needs*, David Fulton, London.

Coulmas, F. (1996), 'Germanness: language and nation', in Stevenson, P. (ed.), *The German Language and the Real World: Sociolinguistic, Cultural and Pragmatic Perspectives on Contemporary German*, Clarendon Press, Oxford.

Council of Europe (1995), *Educational Provision for Traveler and Refugee Pupils: Promoting Achievement*, Council of Europe, Strasbourg.

Council of Europe (1999), *Education in Bosnia and Herzegovina*, Council of Europe, Strasbourg.

Council of Europe (2000a), *The Statute of the Council of Europe (ETS No. 1) 1949*, Accessed 14 February 2000, http://www.coe.fr/eng/legaltxt/1e.htm.

Council of Europe (2000b), *Home Page: List of Member States*. Accessed, 14 February, 2000, http://www.coe.fr/eng/std/states.htm.

Crosby, A. (1997), *The Measure of Reality: Quantification in Western Europe, 1250 - 1600*. Cambridge University Press, Cambridge.

Crow, B. (1983), *Third World Atlas*. Open University Press, Milton Keynes.

Crystal, D. (ed.) (1990), *The Cambridge Encyclopedia*, Cambridge: Cambridge University Press.

Cucos, C. (1997), 'Interculturalism in Romania: the Metamorphosis of a Post-Totalitarian Society', *European Journal of Intercultural Studies* 8, 257-266.

Cunliffe, B. (1997), *The Ancient Celts*. Oxford University Press, Oxford.

Dallin, A. (1981), *German rule in Russia 1941-1945: a Study of Occupation Policies*. London.

Daniels, H. and Garner, P. (eds.) (1999), *World Yearbook of Education 1999: Inclusive Education*. Edited by Coulby, D. and Jones, C. London: Kogan Page.

Davies, N. (1997), *Europe: a History*, Pimlico, London.

Davies, N. (1999), *The Isles: a History*, Macmillan, London.

Department for Education and Employment (1997a), *Excellence for All Children: Meeting Special Educational Needs*, The Stationery Office Limited, London.

Department for Education and Employment (1997b), *Education Action Zones: An Introduction*, Department for Education and Employment, London.

Department for Education and Employment (1998), *Teaching: High Status, High Standards (Circular 4/98)*, Department for Education and Employment, London.

Dieckmann, B. Wulf, C. and Wimmer, M. (eds.) (1997), *Violence - Nationalism, Racism, Xenophobia*, Vol. 5. European Studies in Education. Munster: Waxmann.

Done, K. (1998), 'Unification a slow process', *Financial Tines*, 21.10.98, Survey II.

Doumanis, N. (1998), 'Dodecanese nostalgia for Mussolini's rule', *History Today* 48, 17 - 21.

Doyle, W. (1989), *The Oxford History of the French Revolution*, Oxford University Press, Oxford.

Draculic, S. (1991), *Balkan Express*, Hutchinson, London.

Dragonas, T. Frangoudaki, A. and Inglessi, C. (eds.) (1996), *Beyond One's Own Backyard: Intercultural Teacher Education in Europe*, Athens: Society for the Study of Human Sciences.

Dreifelds, J. (1996), *Latvia in Transition*. Cambridge University Press, Cambridge.

Dunlop, J. (1998), *Russia Confronts Chechnya: Roots of a separatist Conflict*, Cambridge University Press, Cambridge.

Dunstan, J. (1997), *Soviet Schooling in the Second World War*, Macmillan, London.

Eliot, T. S. (1951), *Selected Essays*. 3rd ed. Faber and Faber, London.

Ellis, S. (1997), *Tudor Frontiers and Noble Power: the Making of the British State*, Oxford University Press, Oxford.

Estonia Institute (1995), *Facts about Estonia*. Tallin.

Evans, M. and Lunn, K. (eds.) (1997), *War and Memory in the Twentieth Century*, Oxford: Berg.

Farrow, B. (1999), 'How Hitler conquered Hollywood', *The Guardian Friday Review*, 6 February, 1999, pp. 8-9.

Ferguson, N. (1999), *The Pity of War*, Penguin Books, Harmondsworth.

Ferro, M. (1996), *Colonisation: A Global History*. Trans. Prithipaul, K. P. Routledge, London.

Flouris, G. (1995), 'The Image of Europe in the Curriculum of the Greek Elementary School', in Bell, G. (ed.), *Educating European Citizens: Citizenship, Values and the European Dimension*, David Fulton, London.

Flouris, G. (1996), *Human Rights Education in the Formation of a European Identity: The Case of Greece, England and France*, (unpublished paper).

Ford, J. et al. (1982), *Special Education and Social Control: Invisible Disasters*, Routledge and Kegan Paul, London.

Foucault, M. (1967), *Madness and Civilisation: A History of Insanity in the Age of Reason*, Tavistock, London.

Foucault, M. (1973), *The Birth of the Clinic: An Archaeology of Medical Perception*, Tavistock, London.

Fraction of Kurultaj of Crimean Tater People (1996), 'Principles of restoration of citizenship in the former Soviet States.', in Chubarov, E. (ed.), *Citizen: Information Bulletin # 1 - 2*, 'Assistance' - Foundation on Naturalization and Human Rights, Simferopol, Crimea, Ukraine, pp. 15 - 21.

Freedman, L. (1994), 'General introduction', in Freedman, L. (ed.), *War*. Oxford University Press, Oxford.

Fukuyama, F. (1992), *The End of History and the Last Man*. Hamish Hamilton, London.

Gabrieli, F. (1969), *Arab Historians of the Crusades*. Routledge, London.

Gamini, A. (1999), 'Guns in school draw ovation', *Times Educational Supplement*, 25.

Garner, P. and Sandow, S. (eds.) (1995a), *Advocacy, Self-Advocacy and Special Needs*, London: David Fulton.

Garner, P. and Sandow, S. (1995b), *The Background to Advocacy and Self-Advocacy in the 1990s*, Garner, P. and Sandow, S. (eds.) David Fulton, London.

Geller, D. and Singer, J. D. (1998), *Nations at War: A Scientific Study of International Conflict*, Cambridge University Press, Cambridge.

Gellner, E. (1983), *Nations and Nationalism*, Basil Blackwell, Oxford.

Genninnen, I. (1999), *Reading the Holocaust*, Cambridge University Press, Cambridge.

Giddens, A. (1979), *Central Problems in Social Theory*, Macmillan, London.

Gilbert, M. (1994), *First World War*. Weidenfield and Nicolson, London.

Gillborn, D. and Gipps, C. (1996), *Recent Research on the Achievement of Ethnic Minority Pupils (Ofsted report)*, HMSO for Ofsted, London.

Gillborn, D. and Youdell, D. (2000), *Rationing Education*. Open University Press, Buckingham.

Glaeser, E. (1929), *Class 1902*. Martin Secker, London.

Glass, N. (1999), 'Ministry in dock over racism against gypsies', *Times Educational Supplement*, 25.6.99, p.24.

Gleick, J. (1994), *Genius: Richard Feynman and Modern Physics*, Abacus, London.

Glenny, M. (1996), *The Fall of Yugoslavia*. 3rd ed. Penguin, Harmondsworth.

Glenny, M. (1999), *The Balkans 1804-1999: Nationalism, War and the Great Powers*, Granta Books, London.

Goalen, P. (1997), 'History and national identity in the curriculum', *History Today* 47, 6-9.

Goodenow, R. K. and Marsden, W. E. (1992), *The City and Education in Four Nations*, Cambridge University Press, Cambridge.

Grace, G. (1978), *Teachers, Ideology and Control: A Study in Urban Education*, Routledge and Kegan Paul, London.

Grant, A. and Stringer, K. (eds.) (1995), *Uniting the Kingdom? The Making of British History*. London: Routledge.

Grant, N. (1979), *Soviet Education*. Penguin, Harmondsworth.

Grant, N. (1997), 'Intercultural education in the UK', in Coulby, D. Gundara, J. and Jones, C. (eds.), *The World Yearbook of Education 1997: Intercultural Education*, Kogan Page, London, pp. 178 - 190.

Grant, N. (1999), 'Education in the United Kingdom', in Coulby, D. Cowen, R. and Jones, C. (eds.), *Education in Times of Transition*, Kogan Page, London.

Graves, R. (1929), *Goodbye to All That*. Jonathan Cape, London.

Green, A. (1991), *Education and State Formation. The Rise of Educational Systems in England, France and the USA*. Macmillan, London.

Griffiths, A. Wison-Bareau, J. and Willett, J. (1998), *Disasters of War: Callot, Goya, Dix*. National Touring Exhibitions/Hayward Gallery, London.

The Guardian (1998), 'The Guardian World Cup 98 Guide', *The Guardian*.

Gundara, J. (1997), 'Religion, Secularism and Values Education', in Coulby, D. et al, (eds.), *The World Yearbook of Education 1997*, Kogan Page, London.

Haarmann, H. (1995), 'Multilingualism and Ideology: The Historical Experiment of Soviet Language Politics', *European Journal of Intercultural Studies* 5, 6-17.

Hackett, A (1998), 'Adventist secondary wins funding', *Times Educational Supplement*, 9.6.98, p.11.

Hall, S. et al. (eds.) (1992), *Modernity and its Futures*. Cambridge: Polity Press.

Hargreaves, D. et al. (1975), *Deviance in Classrooms*. Routledge and Kegan Paul, London.

Heaney, S. (1995), *The Redress of Poetry: Oxford Lectures*. Faber and Faber, London.

Hearat, D. (2000), 'Lace curtain spoils Poland's view of EU membership', *The Guardian*, 16.

Heilbronn, R. (1997), *On alleys where they chased a fighter*. (unpublished mss).

Heilbronn, R. (1998), *In Memoriam*. (Unpublished mss).

Heilbronn, R. (1997), 'Refugee education: one in every class', in Heilbronn, R. and Jones, C. (eds.), *New Teachers in an Urban Comprehensive School: Learning in Partnership*, Trentham Books, Stoke-on-Trent.

Heilbronn, R. and Jones, C. (eds.) (1997), *New Teachers in an Urban Comprehensive School: Learning in Partnership*. Stoke-on-Trent: Trentham Books.

Held, D. (1996), *Democracy and the Global Order: From the Modern State to Cosmopolitan Governance*. Polity Press, Cambridge.

Hempton, D. (1996), *Religion and Political Culture in Britain and Ireland: From the Glorious Revolution to the Decline of Empire*. Cambridge University Press, Cambridge.

Hibberd, D. (ed.) (1981), *Poetry of the First World War*. London: Macmillan.

Hickman, M. (1996), *Religion, Class and Identity*. Avebury, Aldershot.

Hicks, D. and Slaughter, R. (eds.) (1998), *The World Yearbook of Education 1998: Futures Education*. The World Yearbook of Education. Edited by Coulby, D. and Jones, C. London: Kogan Page.

Hobsbawm, E. (1990), *Nations and Nationalism since 1780*. Cambridge University Press, Cambridge.

Hobsbawm, E. (1987), *The Age of Empire 1875-1914*. Wiedenfeld and Nicholson, London.

Hogan, M. (ed.) (1996), *Hiroshima in History and Memory*. Cambridge: Cambridge University Press.

Holdsworth, N. (1998), 'Tajiks opt for revival of the fittest', *Times Educational Supplement*, 6.11.98, p.15.

Holsti, K. (1996), *The State, War and the State of War*. Cambridge University Press, Cambridge.

Holsti, K. J. (1991), *Peace and War: Armed Conflicts in International Order, 1648-1989*. Cambridge University Press, Cambridge.

Hope, K. (1998), 'EU outpost looks closer to home', *Financial Times*, 1.6.98, p.I.

Hosking, G. (1998), *Russia: People and Empire, 1552-1917*. Fontana Press, London.

ICIS (International Centre for Intercultural Studies) (2000), *Feasibility Study on the Creation of a South-Eastern European Educational Co-operation Centre (Report to the EU)*. Institute of Education, London University, London.

Ignatieff, N. (1994), *Blood and Belonging: Journeys into the New Nationalism*. Vintage, London.

Illich, I. (1976), *Limits to Medicine: Medical Nemesis: The Expropriation of Health*. Penguin, Harmondsworth.

International Centre for Intercultural Studies (ICIS) (1997), *EU Seminar Report: Refugee Educattion in Europe*. ICIS unpublished report, London.

Irwin, R. (1997), 'Muslim responses to the Crusades', *History Today*, April 1997, pp. 43- 49.

Jabri, V. (1996), *Discourses on Violence; Conflict Analysis Reconsidered*. Manchester University Press, Manchester.

Joint Council for the Welfare of Immigrants (JCWI) (1989), *Unequal Migrants: the European Community's Unequal Treatment of Migrants and Refugees*. Centre for Research in Ethnic Relations, Warwick.

Jones, C. (1993), 'Refugee children in English urban schools', *European Journal of Intercultural Studies* 3, 29-40.

Jones, C. and Rutter, J. (eds.) (1998), *Refugee Education: Mapping the Field*. Stoke-on-Trent: Trentham Books.

Jones, M.(1997), 'Blair's One Nation gambit falters', *The Sunday Times*, 6.4.97, p.1. 11.

Jones, R. A. (1996), *The Politics and Economics of the European Union*. Edward Elgar, Cheltenham.

Joseph, G. G. (1992), *The Crest of the Peacock: Non-European Roots of Mathematics*. Penguin, Harmondsworth.

Joyce, J. (1960), *Ulysses*. Bodley Head, London.

Judah, T. (1997), *The Serbs: History, Myth and the Destruction of Yugoslavia*. Yale University Press, London.

Judah, T. (2000), *Kosovo: War and Revenge*. Yale University Press, New Haven and London.

Kamenska, A. (1995), *The State Language in Latvia: Achievements, Problems and Prospects*. Latvian Centre for Human Rights and Ethnic Studies, Riga.

Kamin, L. J. (1974), *The Science and Politics of IQ*. John Wiley, New York.

Karabel, J. and Halsy, A. H. (1977), *Power and Ideology in Education*. Oxford University Press, New York.

Karaflogka, A. (1997), *Religion, Church and the State in Contemporary Greece: A People's Perspective*, in *IV International Conference on Church-State Relations in Eastern and Central Europe*, Krakow.

Keegan, J. (1993), *A History of Warfare*. Pimlico, London.

Keegan, J. (1997), *The Second World War*. Pimlico, London.

Kennedy, L. (1996), *Colonialism, Religion and Nationalism in Ireland*. Institute of Irish Studies.

Khazanov, A. K. (1995), *After the USSR: Ethnicity, Nationalism and Politics in the Commonwealth of Independent States.* University of Wisconsin Press, Madison.

Kiernan, V. G. (1998), *Colonial Empires and Armies.* War and European Society Best, G. (ed.) Sutton Publishing, Stroud.

Kiev Post (1997), 'From Kuchmese to Kazak, new languages bloom', *Kiev Post*, 13.3.97, p.1 and 4.

Kipling, R. (1923), *Land and Sea Tales for Scouts and Guides.* Macmillan, London.

Kozlov, V. (1988), *The Peoples of the Soviet Union.* Hutchinson, London.

Labov, W. (1969), 'The Logic of Non-Standard English', *Georgetown Monographs on Language and Linguistics* 22, 1-31.

Lahdenpera, P. (1996), 'An analysis of internationalisation and intercultural outlook in Swedish teacher education', *European Journal of Intercultural Studies* 7, 24-34.

Laitin, D. (1996), 'Language and nationalism in the post-Soviet Republics', *Post-Soviet Studies* 12, 4-24.

Lamawaima, K. T. (1995), 'Educating Native Americans', in Banks, J. A. and Banks, C. A. M. (eds.), *Handbook of Research on Multicultural Education*, Macmillan, New York.

Lane, D. (1978), *Politics and Society in the USSR.* Martin Robertson, Oxford.

Lazardis, G. (1996), 'Immigration to Greece: a critical evaluation of Greek policy', *new community,* 22, 335-348.

Leoussi, A. S. (1998), *Nationalism and Classicism: the Classical Body in Nineteenth Century England and France.* Macmillan Press Ltd, Basingstoke.

Lepkowska, D. (1998), 'Muslims gain equality of funding', *Times Educational Supplement*, p. 18.

Lieven, A. (1993), *The Baltic Revolution: Estonia, Latvia, Lithuania and the Path to Independence.* Yale University Press, New Haven.

Lieven, A. (1998), *Chechnya: Tombstone of Russian Power.* Yale University Press, New Haven and London.

Lithuanian Government (undated), *General Concept of Education in Lithuania.* Lithuanian Government, Vilnius.

Maalouf, A. (1984), *The Crusades Through Arab Eyes.* Al Saqu Books, London.

MacGregor, K. (1993), 'Three goals of Mr Ten Percent', *Times Higher Educational Supplement*, 5.3.93, p.12.

Mackey, S. (1997), 'Nationalist hitch to history relaunch', *Times Educational Supplement*, 14.11.97, p.21.

Malcom, N. (1998), *Kosovo: a Short History*. Macmillan, London.

Markou, G. (1997), *The intercultural education and training of teachers*, in *Seminar organised by Democritus University of Thrace and the Friedrich Ebert Stiftung*, The University and Multicultural Societies, Alexandropupolis, Greece.

Massialas, B. G. (1995), *The Quest for a European Identity: The Case of Education in Greece*, in, *Conference of the Comparative and International Education Society*, Boston, Massachusetts.

Mazower, M. (1998), *Dark Continent: Europe's Twentieth Century*. Allen Lane, Harmondsworth.

McDonald, C. (1999), 'Roma in the Romanian Educational System: Barriers and Leaps of Faith', *European Journal of Intercultural Studies (The Education of Roma Children)* 10, 183-200.

McDonald, J. (1998), 'Refugee students' experiences of the UK education system', in Jones, C. and Rutter, J, (eds.), *Refugee Education: Mapping the Field*, Trentham Books, Stoke-on-Trent.

Mestrovic, S. G. (1996), *Genocide After Emotion: The Post-Emotional Balkan War*. Routledge, London.

Microsoft Corporation (1994), *Encarta '95*. Microsoft Corporation, USA.

Miller, L. (1994), *The Educational Needs of Refugee Children in Primary Schools*. London Borough of Greenwich Central Race Equality Unit: Unpublished Report, London.

Miller W. (1995), 'Curbs on asylum-seekers "already too tight"', *The Independent*, 2.

Moretti, F. (1999), *Atlas of the European Novel: 1800-1900*. Verso, London.

Multinacional Culture's Centre (1995), *Multinacionala Multinacional Daugavpils*. Multinacional Culture's Centre, Daugavpils.

Murdoch, A. (1997), 'Why Irish eyes aren't smiling on the great Romanian invasion', *The Independent*, 23.5.97, p.8.

Myrivilis, S. (1987), *Life in the Tomb*. Trans. Bien, P. Quartet Books, London.

Newbolt, H. (1981 (1942)), 'Letter of 2 August 1924 to Margaret Newbolt', in Hibberd, D. (ed.), *Poetry of the First World War*, Macmillan, London.

Nissman, D. and Hill, D. (1997), 'Ukraine: Crimean Turks return late to Latin script', *Crimean Home Page: www.current.nl/users/sota/alfabet.htm*.

Open Society Institute (1996), *Crimean Tatars: Repatriation and Conflict Prevention*. Open Society Institute, New York.

Overy, R. (1998), *Russia's War*. Allen Lane, Harmondsworth.

Park, R. E. Burgess, E. (eds.) (1967), *The City*. Chicago: University of Chicago Press.

Parker, K. and Heindel, A. (1997), *Armed Conflict in the World Today: a Country by Country Review*. Humanitarian Law Project/International Educational Development and Parliamentary Human Rights Group (UK), Los Angeles.

Pavkovic, A. (1996), 'The Yugoslav Idea: A Short History of a Failure', in Perkins, J. and Tampke, J. (eds.), *Europe: Retrospects and Prospects*. South Highlands Publishers, Manly East.

Pavkovic, A. (1997), *The Fragmentation of Yugoslavia: Nationalism in a Multinational State*. Macmillan Press, Basingstoke.

Peieris, R. (1997), *Atomic Histories: A walk through the Beginnings of the Atomic Age with one of its True Pioneers*. American Institute of Physics, New York.

Pesic, V. (1994), 'Bellicose virtues in elementary school readers', in Rosandic, R. and Pesic, V. (eds.), *Warfare, Patriotism, Patriarchy: The Analysis of Elementary School Textbooks*. Centre for Anti-war Action MOST, Belgrade.

Pettifer (1994), *The Greeks: The Land and the People Since the War*. Penguin, Harmondsworth.

Pinder, D. (ed.) (1998), *The New Europe: Economy, Society and Environment*. Chichester: John Wiley.

Pine, L. (1997a), 'The dissemination of Nazi ideology and family values through school textbooks', *History of Education*, 25, 91 - 109.

Pine, L. (1997b), 'Nazism in the classroom', *History Today*, April 1997, 22 - 27.

Piskun, O. (1996), 'Institution of Citizenship in Ukraine', *Migration Issues*, 1, 16-18.

Psomiades, H. and Thomadaki, S. (1993), 'Greece, the New Europe and the Changing International order', in,,, Pella Publications, New York.

Reid, A. (1998), *Borderland: a Journey through the History of Ukraine*. Phoenix, London.

Reid, E. (1997), 'Education and linguistic diversity', in Coulby, D. Gundara, J. and Jones, C. (eds.), *The World Yearbook of Education 1997: Intercultural Education*, Kogan Page, London, pp. 27-38.

Remarque, E. M. (1929), *All Quiet on the Western front*. Putnam, London.

Rhodes, R. (1987), *The making of the Atomic Bomb*. Simon and Schuster, New York.

Roberts, D. (1996), *Minds at War: the Poetry and Experience of the First World War*. Saxon Books, Burgess Hill.

Robinson, M. (1995), *Opinion.* BBC Radio 4, 14 September 1995, London.

Romains, J. (1939), *Verdun.* Peter Davies, London.

Romaniszyn, K. (1996), 'The invisible community: undocumented Polish workers in Athens', *new community* 23, 321-333.

Rosandic, R. and Pesic, V. (1994), *Warfare, Patriotism, Patriarchy: The Analysis of Elementary School Textbooks.* Centre for Anti-war Action MOST, Belgrade.

Roscoe, J. (1914), *The Ethics of War, Spying and Military Training.* David Nutt, London.

Roshwald, A. and Stites, R. (eds.) (1999), *European Culture in the Great War: the Arts, Entertainment and Propaganda, 1914-1918.* Studies in the Social and Cultural History of Modern Warfare, 7. Cambridge: Cambridge University Press.

Rudge, L. (1998), '"I am nothing" - Does it Matter? A Critique of Current Religious Education Policy and Practice in England on Behalf of the Silent Majority', *British Journal of Religious Education* 20, 155-165.

Runciman, S. (1965), *A History of the Crusades. Volume 1: The First Crusade and the Foundation of the Kingdom of Jerusalem.* Penguin Books, Harmondsworth.

Russell, J. (c.1838), *A Complete Atlas of the World.* Fischer Son and Co, London.

Rutter, J. (1994), *Refugee Children in the Classroom.* Trentham Books, Stoke-on-Trent.

Rutter, J. (1997), *We Left Because We Had To.* Second ed. Refugee Council, London.

Rutter, J. (1998), 'Refugees in today's world', in Jones, C. and Rutter, J. (eds.), *Refugee Education: Mapping the Field*, Trentham Books, Stoke-on-Trent, pp. 13 - 32.

Sammons, P. Thomas, S. Mortimore, P. et al. (1994), *Assessing School Effectiveness: Developing Measures to put School Performance in Context.* Office for Standards in Education (OFSTED), London.

Sandow, S. (1994), *Whose Special Need? Some Perceptions of Special Educational Needs.* Paul Chapman, London.

Sarwar, G. (1993), *British Muslims and Schools.* The Muslim Education Trust, London.

Sassoon, S. (1928), *Memoirs of a Fox-hunting Man.* Faber and Faber, London.

Sassoon, S. (1930), *Memoirs of an Infantry Officer.* Faber and Faber, London.

Sassoon, S. (1936), *Sherston's Progress*. Faber and Faber, London.

Sassoon, S. (1945), *Siegried's Journey 1916 - 1920*. Faber and Faber, London.

Sells, M. A. (1996), *The Bridge Betrayed: Religion and Genocide in Bosnia*. University of California Press, San Francisco.

Shakespeare, W. (1949), *Shakespeare's King Lear: a Critical Edition. (Edited by G. I. Duthrie)*. OUP, Oxford.

Shakespeare, W. (1997), *King Lear. Arden Shakespeare Third Series*. Foakes, W. (ed.) Routledge, London.

Sharma, S. (1991), *The Embarrassment of Riches*. Fontana Press, London.

Silova, I. (1996), 'De-Sovietisation of Russian Textbooks Made Visible', *European Journal of Intercultural Studies* 7, 35-45.

Simon, B. (1971), *Intelligence, Psychology and Education: A Marxist Critique*. Lawrence and Wishart, London.

Smith, K. and Benson, J. (eds.) (1993), *Klaonica: Poems for Bosnia*. Newcastle upon Tyne: Bloodaxe Books.

Solchanyk, R. (1993), 'The Politics of Language in Ukraine', *RFE/RL Research Report* 2, 1-4.

Stackelberg, R. (1999), *Hitler's Germany: Origins, Interpretations, Legacies*. Routledge, London and New York.

Staunton, D. (1998), 'File reopened on German arson attack', *The Guardian*, 9.4.98, p. 15.

Stojanovic, D. (1994), 'History text books mirror their time', in Rosandic, R. and Pesic, V. (eds.), *Warfare, Patriotism, Patriarchy: The Analysis of Elementary School Textbooks*, Centre for Anti War Action MOST, Belgrade.

Supple, C. (1993), *From Prejudice to Genocide: Learning about the Holocaust*. Trentham, London.

Szasz, T. S. (1972), *The Myth of Mental Illness*. Paladin, St Albans.

Tate, N. (1996), 'Culture is not anarchy', *The Times*, 8.2.96, p.18.

Teacher Training Agency (2000), *Raising the Attainment of Minority Ethnic Pupils: guidance and resource material for providers of initial teacher training*. Teacher Training Agency, London.

The Royal Ministry of Education; Research and Church Affairs (Norway) (1997), *Core Curriculum for Primary, Secondary and Adult Education in Norway*. National Centre for Educational Resources, Oslo.

The Times (1991), *The Times Atlas of the World: Family Edition*. Times Books, London.

Thomas, E. (1981 (1914)), 'War poetry', in Hibberd, D. (ed.), *Poetry of the First World War*, Macmillan, London.

Thompson, A. (1997), 'Major to call on teenagers to join cadets', *The Times*, 23.1.97, p.1.

Tomlinson, S. (1981), *Educational Subnormality - A Study in Decision Making*. Routledge and Kegan Paul, London.

Tomlinson, S. (1982), *A Sociology of Special Education*. Routledge and Kegan Paul, London.

UNDP (United Nations Development Programme) (1995), *Latvia Human Development Report*. Riga

UNHCR (United Nations High Commissioner for Refugees) (1997), 'The year in review', *Refugee Magazine* III - 1997, 1-31.

United Nations (2000), *Home Page: List of Member States*. Accessed 14 February, 2000, http://www.un.org/Overview/unmember.html.

United Nations High Commissioner for Refugees in Ukraine (1997), 'United Nations High Commissioner for Refugees in Ukraine', *Migration Studies: Ukrainian Analytical-Informative Journal* 2, 32 - 36.

Vallely, P. (1997), 'Creative tension', *The Independent Tabloid*, 8.4.97, p.1-2.

Vaughan, M. (1969), 'The Grandes Ecoles', in Wilkinson, R. (ed.), *Governing Elites: Studies in Training and Selection*, Oxford University Press, New York.

Vipotnik, M. (1998), 'Clash proved case for EU', *Financial Times*, 6.7.98, p. Survey 8.

Vipotnik, M. (1998), 'Constant Source of Friction', *Financial Times*, 6.7.98, p. Survey 7.

Wallensteen, P. and Axell, K. (1993), 'Armed conflict at the end of the Cold War, 1989-92', *Journal of Peace Research* 10.

Ward, M. H. (1917), *Towards the Goal*. John Murray, London.

Weinberg, G. (1994), *A World at Arms: a Global History of World War II*. Cambridge University Press, Cambridge.

Westwood, S. (1994), 'Racism, Mental Illness and the Politics of Identity', in Rattansi, A. W. S. (ed.), *Racisms, Modernity and identity: On the Western Front*, Polity Press, London.

Wilkinson, R. (ed.) (1969), *Governing Elites: Studies in Training and Selection*. New York: Oxford University Press.

Williams, R. (1957), *Culture and Society*. Chatto and Windus, London.

Williams, R. (1961), *The Long Revolution*. Chatto and Windus, London.

Wilson, A. (1993), 'Crimea's political cauldron', *RFE/RL Research Report*.

Winter, J. (1998), *Sites of Memory, Sites of Mourning: The Great War in European Cultural History*. Cambridge University Press/Canto, Cambridge.

Winter, J. and Robert, J-L. (eds.) (1999), *Capital Cities at War: Paris, London, Berlin 1914-1919*. Studies in the Social and Cultural History of Modern Warfare, 2. Cambridge: Cambridge University Press.

Winter, J. and Sivan, E. (eds.) (1999), *War and Rememberance in the Twentieth Century*. Studies in the Social and Cultural History of Modern Warfare, 5. Cambridge: Cambridge University Press.

Yevtushenko, Y. (1966), *The Poetry of Yevgeny Yevtushenko: 1953-1963*. Trans. Reavey, G. Calder and Boyars, London.

Young, R. (1990), *White Mythologies: Writing History and the West*. Routledge, London.

Young, R. (1996), 'MI6 advice stops academic book', *The Times*, 3.2.96, p.4.

Young, R. J. C. (1995), *Colonial Desire: Hybridity in Theory, Culture and Race*. Routledge, London.

Yule, W. (1998), 'The psychological adaptation of refugee children.' in Jones, C. and Rutter, J. (eds.), *Refugee Education: Mapping the Field*, Trentham Books, Stoke-on-Trent.

Zambeta, A. (2000), *Public Discourse on Education Governanace, Social Inclusion and Exclusion: Political Actors in Greek Education*. Athens

Zambeta, E. (1999), *Crisis and Reform in Greek Education - A Text Analysis of Law 2525/1997*. Athens

Zubarev, V. (1996), 'The role of NGOs in rendering assistance to former deported peoples, which come back', in Chubarov, E. (ed.), *Citizen: Information Bulletin # 1 - 2*, 'Assistance' - Foundation on Naturalization and Human Rights, Simferopol, Crimea, Ukraine, pp. 4-7.

Zujiene, I. (1995), 'Education in Lithuania - An Object of Reform', in Wulf, C. (ed.), *Education in Europe: An Intercultural Task*, Waxmann, Munster.

Index